THE LEADERSHIP BOOK

The Leadership Book

by
Charles J. Keating

PAULIST PRESS
New York/Ramsey/Toronto

Library of Congress
Catalog Card Number: 77-99300

ISBN: 0-8091-2090-9

Published by Paulist Press
Editorial Office: 1865 Broadway, New York, N.Y. 10023
Business Office: 545 Island Road, Ramsey, N.J. 07446

Printed and bound in the
United States of America

Contents

Introduction..1

1. The Dilemmas of Leadership...........................5

2. The Two Dimensions of Leadership 23

3. Leadership: Reading the Group 38

4. Leadership: Handling Conflict.......................54

5. Improving Our Leadership Style 71

6. Leadership and Decision Making....................85

7. Leadership and Planning 103

8. Leadership and Management.......................116

9. Christian Leadership 127

*To
Kate,
my partner, my friend,
my wife*

Introduction

The Leadership Book is written for the new leader who is faced with lots of exciting challenges and for the experienced leader who often suspects he or she could lead better. It is written for leaders in the Church, especially leaders at the local level of diocese, parish or prayer group.

The first two chapters will deal with some personal dimensions of the leader: the assumptions we make about leadership and about people, the assumptions we make about ourselves and styles of behavior that influence our leadership style. Together, we shall explore some of the options open to leadership and the importance of a leader's judgment. We shall discuss the most recent studies of leadership and their practical application to Church leadership.

With chapter 3 the "how to" of leadership will be discussed. Some theories of group development and its significance for the leader will form a backdrop for practical suggestions affecting leadership. How to handle conflict and to improve our leadership style are the topics of chapters 4 and 5.

Chapters 6, 7 and 8 offer some techniques and structures for accomplishing work in a group or community. Thanks to current research and experimentation we now have available to us techniques for community or group decision making, for long and short range community planning and for effective management with which the effective leader needs to be acquainted.

Chapter 9 will focus on Christian leadership, a theme that regularly surfaces throughout the book.

Can the Christian leader in the Church be an effective leader without human skills? Leaving aside for the moment the occasional prophet and charismatic leader, I do not believe so. Without the human skills of leadership, the most devout of Christian leaders can offer only mediocre leadership. True, some leaders seem to have the human skills for working with people and motivating them from birth. Most of us have to acquire the skills. But the point is that whether we have the skills naturally or through painful acquisition, there is no leadership without them. God gave Aaron to Moses because Moses stuttered; He assured Jeremiah that he could do His work in spite of his youth. Scripture abounds with God's supplying for human deficiencies. But for most of us in leadership positions in the Church today, He does not do so. Most of us have to do our own supplying if we want to facilitate the work of the Spirit of Jesus through ourselves.

A basic premise of this book is that there is no such thing as the purely human for the believer. We are made, and the world has been made and sustained, in the image of the Son of God, the Word through whom the Father made all things. The only real world is a Christ-ed world. Sin, therefore, is not human, but a distortion of humanity corrected and made whole by the visible entry of the Son into His creation, in Jesus. In this sense, all that is human is good.

Another basic premise of this book is that the Incarnation needs to be taken seriously. Jesus took human nature seriously enough to share it with us. He used human skills to begin the restoration of all things in Himself. He did not leave salvation to prayer and spirituality alone. It seems to me that we have not yet grasped the resounding implications of taking the Incarnation seriously; we have not yet become convinced that the human is as important as the divine for the coming of the Kingdom, that the skill of community decision making and the skill of management are as indispensable as the skill of prayer and the skill of charity if we are to "complete His work on earth." (Eucharistic Prayer IV)

I have written this book with the conviction that since the human sciences (arts?) such as psychology, sociology, anthropology and the behavioral sciences focus on the human person and his or her nature, and since God's revelation is to the human person and his or her community with its accompanying human nature, in the world of the believer the findings of the human sciences and the Word of revelation are equally important. Since both focus on the same human nature, both could be more effective by listening to the other. The beneficiary of such mutual listening would be people, whom both purport to benefit in the first place.

Most of us who find ourselves in positions of Church leadership, especially those of us in such humbler positions, find that we have had little, if any, specific training for such positions. If we founder and sink, some will say that such positions should never be occupied by "laymen" or "the young" or "women." These remarks are usually made by the opposite life positions: "cleric" or "elderly" or "men." If we succeed, it is often taken for granted. I believe that, in most instances, success or failure is determined by having skills of leadership or not. And for most of us leadership like parenthood is a learned skill.

Chapter 1
The Dilemmas of Leadership

Am I a leader? Do I want to be a leader? What is leadership? Who gives leadership? Why do we need leadership? Or do we? What goes into leadership? How do I know if I'm a good leader? What is a *good* leader? Are there special skills a leader needs? Are there different *kinds* of leadership? Can I always be a leader? How can I be a better leader? How can I get things done quickly without leaving others behind? Is a *Christian* leader different from other leaders? Does Jesus always model leadership for me?

In the past two and a half decades leadership has gone through a series of changes. Writing in 1960, Alex Bavelas, a successful behavioral scientist, summed up the studies on leadership of the previous decade: "Early notions about leadership were explicitly associated with special powers. An outstanding leader was credited not only with extensions of the normal abilities possessed by most men, but with extraordinary powers, such as the ability to read men's minds, to tell the future, to compel obedience hypnotically." ("Leadership: Man and Function," *Administrative Science Quarterly*, March 1960, IV, no. 4, p. 491) Today, leadership is related more to particular situations: a man or woman might be a leader in one situation, but not in another; the leader of an African safari might not be able to lead a parish, and vice versa. Cardinal Leger and Archbishop Sheen are strong leaders, but only in their own particular situations. Golda Meir was a strong leader, until the situation changed; DeGaulle rose and fell as a leader with the changes of French politics. All of us know of pastors who showed extraordinary leadership in one parish but not in another. Today's research indicates that leadership rests in judgment, the ability to judge accurately the needs of a group, and in the skill to fill those needs. In addition, leadership needs to be seen as leadership by others; it does not exist in a vacuum. (Cf. "So You Want To Know Your Leadership Style?" *Training and Development Journal*, February 1974, pp. 20-37)

By the end of this book, all of the questions at the opening of this chapter will be answered. In this chapter, I want to concentrate on some of the more recent theories of leadership, getting into ways to improve our own leadership ability in the following chapters. If you are not a "theory person," you might want to skip ahead and come back to this chapter at your leisure. In other words, read this book in a way that is most helpful to you.

The Leader's Assumptions

The source of the dilemmas of leadership can often be found in the leader's assumptions about himself or herself, about people in general and about the situation. These incline the leader to one or another particular style of leadership. The leader may have grown up in a competitive environment; the livelihood of the lay parish leader may require that he be competitive. When the leader finds himself or herself at the head of a group that needs an environment of cooperation, he or she may find himself or herself in a dilemma. We are pressured to get the job done, but we sense that it is important that all points of view be heard, and that takes time. We are used to leading in a business world in which the livelihood of the followers can be at stake, but we find ourselves at the head of a volunteer group who are giving more than getting. We feel comfortable making decisions for the group, but we suspect that group decision making and consensus would be more effective. What to do? How to do it?

The leader has several options. Warren Schmidt and Robert Tannenbaum of California have placed these options on a continuum:

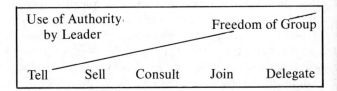

Use of Authority by Leader				Freedom of Group
Tell	Sell	Consult	Join	Delegate

Moving from left to right on the continuum lessens the directive authority of the leader and increases the freedom of the group. No one option is good or bad. Each one *can be appropriate*, depending upon the leader, the group and the situation. If the leader chooses to *tell* the group, he or she reviews the facts, makes a decision and informs the group of his or her decision. If he or she *sells* the group, he or she does the same, but goes one step further: he or she persuades the group to accept his or her decision, giving its reasoning and valuable consequences, etc. The leader who *consults* the group presents the issue to them, accepts possible solutions and alternatives, then makes the decision himself or herself. When the leader *joins* the group he or she presents the issue and defines the limits within which a solution needs to be found; together they then study alternative solutions and come to a group solution. To *delegate* to the group, the leader presents them with the issue and defines the limits of a possible solution; the group then studies the various alternatives and arrives at a decision, which the leader accepts. There are, of course, extremes on both sides of the continuum. To the left is the "autocrat," whose domineering style violates our self-image of people who are open and sensitive; to the right is the "abdicrat," who leads by abdicating, being irresponsible and violating concepts of leadership that gets work done. It is likely that neither of these is a leader in any effective way; he or she is a dictator or a playboy or playgirl. Both may have authority, but not leadership. I shall speak about the difference between authority and leadership later in this chapter, when we review another theory of leadership.

Confusion about the kind of leadership being given can be destructive. The Detroit "Call to Action" conference may be a case in point. The delegates to this bicentennial event seemed to understand that they were being *delegated* to arrive at decisions that the bishops who delegated them would accept. The bishops, on the other hand, seemed to understand themselves as *consulting*, reserving the right to make any decisions. The consequence has been disappointment and lack of confidence on both sides. Confusion at the leadership level is costly.

Both the leader and the led need to know what kind of leadership is being exercised. And the choice of leadership styles depends on several things. It depends on the leader's own self-concept, his or her awareness of his or her own needs, and his or her assumptions about people. He or she has to be aware of his or her motives and values, of the level of confidence he or she has in the group, of the leadership style to which he or she is inclined because he or she is most comfortable and successful with it, of his or her own feelings of security and tolerance for ambiguity, and of his or her own perceptions of the task to be done.

The leader, for instance, who sees his or her appointment as a reward for work well done or for other favors will perceive the task of the group quite differently than the leader whose appointment has come from a deep commitment to the group's purpose. The insecure leader will spend a good deal of time in a defensive posture with the group, while the secure leader will be more comfortable handling group conflict and living with ambiguity. The leader who has found success with democratic styles of leadership will function differently than the more directive leader. The leader needs self-knowledge.

The leader's assumptions about people also affect his or her choice of options. Abraham H. Maslow, a famous researcher of motivation, discovered that we have a hierarchy of needs:

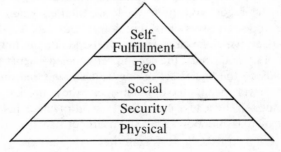

Physical needs are those concerned with survival: food, shelter, etc. Security needs have to do with protecting the means of survival: resting safe with what we need to live. Social needs are needs of belonging and fitting into life with others. Our ego needs look for personal recognition and approval from others. Self-fulfillment needs include the internalization of our convictions, doing what we do because we want to do it, rather than because we have to do it to live or because it is the law. Maslow found that until more basic needs were met, the physical and security needs, a person was not motivated by the higher needs of social, ego or self-fulfillment. Victims of a hurricane, for instance, are not likely to want to attend a self-development workshop; they need to be fed and housed and to regain some security. But Maslow also discovered that once the more basic needs were met, appeals to them no longer motivated; only appeals to the higher needs spurred people to act. So, for instance, those who are fulfilled at the security level will not be attracted by additional insurance policies, but they might be motivated by an invitation to a significant community banquet, since this would appeal to their social needs.

The leader's assumptions about the needs of people colors his or her assumption about them. Douglas McGregor built upon Maslow's findings when he developed two sets of assumptions about people. The first set, which he calls Theory X, builds on the lower set of human needs; the second set, labeled Theory Y, builds on the higher set of needs, assuming that once the lower needs have been met, they no longer motivate. The leader may find it useful to check his or her own assumptions against McGregor's theories.

Theory X

1. The average human being has an inherent dislike of work and will avoid it if he or she can.
2. Because of this human characteristic of dislike of work, most people have to be coerced, controlled, directed, and threatened with punishment to get them to put forth adequate effort toward the achievement of results.
3. The average human being prefers to be directed, wishes to avoid responsibility, has relatively little ambition, and wants security above all.

Theory Y

1. The expenditure of physical and mental effort in work is as natural as play or rest.
2. External control and the threat of punishment are not the only means for bringing about effort toward results. Men and women will exercise self-direction and self-control in the service of objectives to which they are committed.
3. Commitment to objectives is related to the rewards associated with their achievement.
4. The average human being learns, under proper conditions, not only to accept but to seek responsibility.
5. The capacity to exercise a relatively high degree of imagination, ingenuity, and creativity in the solution of problems is widely, not narrowly, distributed in the population.
6. Under the conditions of modern, industrial life, the intellectual potentialities of the average human being are only partially utilized. (Cf.

The Human Side of Enterprise, McGraw-Hill,
N.Y., 1958)

The need for the leader is not to determine which side
is "right," but to do some reflection that indicates to
him or her that his or her assumptions affect his or her
behavior. He or she can then choose whether to retain
those assumptions as helpful or to re-examine them.
Most of us probably are a mixture of Theory X and
Theory Y assumptions.

My self-knowledge as a leader and my assumptions about others influence my reading of my group
and my choice of options. They influence how I read
the group's need for independence or dependence,
their readiness to assume responsibility, their tolerance for ambiguity, their interest in the problem, their
commitment to it, their expectations of involvement in
the solution of the issue, their competencies and ca-
pacities to better these, and the effect on the group
created by my assumptions and resultant behavior.

Effective leadership needs to know itself, needs to
know its followers, and needs to know the situation. In
the situation we look at what kind of a group, parish or
system we are dealing with, the pressures of time, the
effect of our actions upon other individuals, groups,
parishes or systems, and the perceptions that I, the
group, and others have of our task. We need, in other
words, to have as clear a picture as possible of ourselves and our environment.

Ideally, the leader would then choose the option
that would be most effective for results and satisfaction. He or she may be limited in options because of
his or her comfort with one or another style of leader-

ship and discomfort or disbelief in another. In the long range, however, the goal of leadership is to be able to choose and use that option that the group now needs.

The Leader's Perceptions

It has long been thought that the determination of what a group needs from a leader depended largely on the acute and accurate perceptions of the leader. The ability to judge a group, to determine its level of maturity, is still, no doubt, the key to offering effective leadership. A fifteen-year study by Fred E. Fiedler of the University of Illinois, however, suggests that the attitude or expectations of the leader also play a crucial role in effective leadership. (Cf. *A Theory of Leadership Effectiveness*, McGraw-Hill, N.Y. 1967) A major outcome of Fiedler's study was the discovery that *reality* has little to do with good leader-member relationships because it has little to do with good interpersonal relationships! It makes little difference whether a person is sensitive or responsive or cooperative *in reality;* what makes the difference is *my view* of him or her as sensitive, responsive or cooperative. It makes little difference whether my view is accurate or not. Fiedler sums it up in this way:

> The underlying assumption, especially in lay circles and in some training programs, has been that accuracy in perception is a prerequisite, or at least a highly desirable attribute, of the good interpersonal relationship. However, there is little evidence to support this view. In fact, accurate, ob-

jective but unfavorable perceptions may be less desirable for many good relationships than inaccurate but favorable perceptions. Most people want to be accepted for what they would like to be, not for what they really are. (*ibid.*, p. 39)

In the next chapter we shall reflect on the role that interpersonal relationships play in making a leader effective. For the moment it is only important to recognize the difficulty of truly "reading" others. A recent professional study of a religious order in a monastery underlined the difficulty that even such a close group of men found in knowing whether they were liked or disliked, tolerated or appreciated by the others in any objective way. Our perceptions of others and of ourselves are more often misperceptions and wishful thinking. Strangely enough, such wishful thinking has a greater impact on our relationships with others than any acutely objective insights!

If Fiedler's findings are accurate, and they ring true for me, our expectations of others affect our leadership effectiveness. Perhaps it is a phenomenon not far from the "wish-fulfilling-prophecy" in which we get what we expect. The effective leader sees a favorable likeness between himself or herself and others, even between himself or herself and those that he or she would least like to work with or live with. Such a leader seems to be able to distinguish between the *person*, whom he or she views favorably, and the *performance* or *job* of the person, which he or she recognizes as below par or inferior in quality. The less effective leader and the ineffective leader do not make this distinction. Their evaluation of a task poorly done is also

an evaluation of a person as insensitive, uncoopera-
tive, etc.

On the other hand, some misperceptions and misconceptions can be very destructive to the leader's
effectiveness. One of my findings has been that many
people conjure up a picture of power and repression
when "leadership" is mentioned. They see long lines
of people who are the same, all differences and devi-
ations being suppressed. They picture the drill
sergeant! Many still think of the leader as the specially
gifted person described earlier in this chapter by Alex
Bavelas. For them a born leader is one who demon-
strates that he or she has those special gifts. In the
Christian community leadership is rightly seen as a
charism, but it is a charism that can be poisoned by
misconceptions. In short, a favorable but mistaken
view of others helps to make leadership effective; a
distorted view of leadership can make it very ineffective.

In one charismatic core group I know of, such
distorted views of leadership were harmful to the
group as well as to the people involved. In this group
there was a growing struggle for leadership between
two men, one a layman and the other a priest. The
conflict was over the power to influence the direction
of the group; each man disagreed regularly with the
other and vied for the support of the other members of
the group. Each seemed to understand leadership in
terms of having his own ideas accepted and imposing
his will on the group. Each seemed to have the natural
abilities that would normally equip him for leadership
and each felt the charism of leadership. Over a period
of several months, the priest pressed less and less,

but, in the end, the layman was not accepted by the group. He eventually left it and the Catholic Church as well. It was a sad story; a more accurate conception of leadership as a service could have prevented it.

Leadership as Service

Current writers and researchers of leadership tend to define it as a process of influencing the activities of an individual or group in efforts toward accomplishing goals in a given situation. (Cf. Paul Hersey and Kenneth H. Blanchard, *Management of Organizational Behavior*, 2nd edition, Prentice-Hall, N.Y., 1972, p. 68) There are three important dimensions, then, to leadership: it is situational, it is a service, and it needs to be perceived as leadership *by others*.

Leadership is situational, largely depending upon the needs of others and even influenced by the needs of the leader himself or herself. Leadership styles need to change from group to group and situation to situation. The leader's style changes when he or she personally changes. In the above example, for instance, both the layman and the priest seemed to have misread the needs of the core group: the group was more mature and less open to directive styles of leadership than was thought. In a less mature group such directive styles of leadership might have been effective, provided, of course, that the conflict level could have been maintained at a tolerable balance.

Leadership is service, in the sense that it seeks to meet the needs of another or of the group by performing needed functions. Sometimes strong directive power is effective leadership, such as when a group has lost its sense of direction or purpose; with another group, or at another time when the group is functioning well in its relationships and has its directions clear, non-directive styles of leadership are needed. Sometimes the group needs to be encouraged and supported; at other times it may need to be reoriented. Leadership serves the need of the group. In this sense, leadership may be exercised by any group member at any time; a designated leader might have power or authority, but leadership functions do not belong to him or her alone. In fact, a mark of leadership for the designated leader is the success with which he or she encourages other group members to exercise leadership functions. In this way the designated leader facilitates the maturity of the group.

The service of leadership blends two concerns: concern for the job to be done and concern for the relationships between the people involved. It is a *task function* to contribute to the completion of the job. It is a *relationship function* to contribute to smooth human relationships between the people doing the job. At one time or another every group needs something of both; each is a leadership function.

Some examples of task functions are:

Initiating	ANY ATTEMPT TO GET AN ACTION OR MOVEMENT STARTED. Suggesting a new direction for the group discussion or offering a way to get the discussion going.
Regulating	ATTEMPTS TO ORDER THE DIRECTION AND PACE OF THE GROUP. Calling attention to time,

mentioning the agenda, suggesting a structure to go about the task, recalling the group from a tangent.

Informing GIVING OR SOLICITING INFORMATION. Giving opinions, asking opinions, reporting data, asking for data.

Supporting BUILDING ON THE IDEAS OF ANOTHER. Supporting another's suggestions or initiations with additional input. Elaborating on the thoughts of another, acknowledging the contributions of another by adding to them.

Evaluating CRITIQUING THE FEASIBILITY OF AN IDEA. Testing the group for consensus, examining the practicality of a suggestion, helping the group to look at its own process for critique.

Summarizing DIGESTING THE DISCUSSION OF THE GROUP AT SOME POINT. Sharing with the group what you hear them saying, restating the contributions of another for clarity.

Some examples of the relationship functions are:

Encouraging BEING FRIENDLY, WARM, APPROVING. Telling another you like his or her ideas, smiling or nodding approval, asking another to say more about his or her idea.

Expressing Feelings	SHARING ONE'S OWN FEELINGS OR THE FEELINGS ONE SENSES IN THE GROUP. Expressing your pleasure in working with the group, pointing out that you feel a tension in the group.
Harmonizing	ATTEMPTS TO RECONCILE DISAGREEMENTS BETWEEN OTHERS. Getting people to explore their differences, pointing out where you see agreement.
Compromising	MODIFYING ONE'S OWN OPINION OR FEELINGS FOR THE GOOD OF THE GROUP. Admitting error, disciplining oneself to help maintain group cohesion, disciplining oneself to stay at the pace of the group.
Gatekeeping	FACILITATING THE PARTICIPATION OF OTHERS. Seeking the view of a less vocal participant, suggesting ways that the opinions of all might be expressed, any effort to "open the gate" to fuller use of the group's resources.
Setting Standards	EXPRESSING NORMS BY WHICH THE GROUP MAY OPERATE. Offering ground rules for working together, suggesting ways to evaluate the human dynamics of the group, challenging the group to use time or structures better.

Not all of these functions are needed every time a

group meets, but in the long run all will be needed. Used well, they can remove obstacles to communication, understanding and the work of the Spirit. God speaks through the prophet on occasion, but not every leader is a prophet; rather the Christian leader believes that God's Word is found in the Christian community. It is the community that preserves God's Word. (Cf. Vatican Council II, *Dogmatic Constitution on Divine Revelation*, par. 8) We need to have the human skills of listening and dialogue to open the potential of the community to express, specify and apply His Word to our concerns. That is to be incarnational; that is Christian leadership. To paraphrase an earlier wisdom, the Christian leader needs to live under the dictum "I am Christian, and nothing human is foreign to me!"

A third dimension of leadership as service is that it needs always to be a consistent set of influencing or serving behaviors *as perceived by others*. Since others must recognize leadership as service, leadership is essentially in our behavior. Intentions are important for our integrity and honesty, but they do not lead. The leader has to be recognized and accepted as a leader *by others* whom he or she seeks to lead. If the "leader" is not so perceived by the followers, he or she might have power or authority, but he or she is not a leader.

The Archdiocese of Newark, in recently issued parish council guidelines, specifies these three dimensions of leadership. I shall review the guidelines in greater detail in chapter 8, but it is well to note here what they say about the president of the council as leader. The guidelines note that "much of the president's work takes place outside of actual meetings." It is the president's function to facilitate and insure communication with the pastor, pastoral team, committee chairpersons, other council officers and parishioners. He or she needs to see that council members make use of resources and training programs. He or she is responsible for the functioning of the executive committee. It is valuable to be clear about what is expected of one's office; it can also be intimidating. I believe that only if the president sees his or her role as one of service will he or she have the courage and the style to carry it off successfully. The community needs this work done. Other leaders in the community fill other needs. If it is done as a service, it will be Christian. The Christian community needs Christian leadership. The dilemmas of leadership need not discourage such service.

Summary

Leadership is a process of facilitating the goal achievement of an individual or of a group in a particular situation. Because leadership is human, even in a church community, it must deal with the complexity of human beings. The leader needs to know himself or herself, his or her needs and motives; he or she needs to know the assumptions that he or she makes about people, because these will show in his or her behavior; he or she needs to recognize the fallibility of his or her perceptions, when to trust them and when to question them; he or she needs to know the situation into which he or she will channel his or her leadership functions and train others to do the same. Most of all, if he or she chooses or is chosen to lead, he or she needs to serve.

In the next chapter I shall suggest ways in which we can grow to give the kind of service that the Christian community needs and deserves. Particularly, we shall explore in greater detail various kinds of leadership styles and the situations in which they are most productive. Stephen B. Clark, in his book *Building Christian Community*, suggested that one of the tasks of today's Christian leader was to offer a "vision" to his or her followers. We shall reflect on that also.

Chapter 2
The Two Dimensions of Leadership

Bart Jones was a successful businessman, a pioneer, almost, in the way he could open up new avenues of sale and maintain them against heavy competition. He was religious, too. He and his family gave freely of their time and effort to the new parish in which they found themselves. In fact, it was Bart who was largely responsible for the vitality and popularity of the new parish council. And he was recognized. He was the first president of the council. Under his direction, funds were raised for the construction of a parish center before the first brick was laid. By the time the last brick was laid the center was paid for and a parish banquet was held to celebrate, a banquet that proved to be so successful that it still remains an annual affair.

When Bart had to move on and settle elsewhere in the state because of his expanding business and the creation of a new, more centralized, headquarters, he moved into a well-established parish, one that was almost meeting the needs of its parishioners and would have met them entirely if more people and money were available. One of the outstanding things about the parish was its parish council; the members worked well together, easily integrated new members into its structure, and was productive enough to be admired by the local community. "It knows what it's doing" was not an infrequent remark. It provided with vigor economic, social and spiritual service to the parish and often to the community. Bart's reputation had preceded him and he was welcomed with open arms. Eventually, he was elected to the council and then to its presidency. Using the strong, directive style of leadership with which he felt comfortable, and which had been so successful in his previous parish, Bart experienced small, but growing, problems. Conflict gradually increased between himself and parish committees, attendance at meetings slowly dropped off, and he found himself and his family doing much of the work that, he thought, others had done under the previous president. The time and pressure began to show in his business dealings, so he resigned before the end of his term as council president. He was mystified: he had been so successful before; what had happened?

The Functions of Leadership

As we saw in our last chapter, many things could have happened. Bart may not have known himself well enough, his needs and motives; he may not have examined his assumptions about people so that he could modify them in the light of his new experience; he may not have taken into account sufficiently the differences between the two parishes; his service may not have been seen as service by others. Some of the mystery, however, might be resolved if we look more closely at the task and relationship functions described in chapter 1.

Certain things need to happen in a group to keep or make it productive and to keep it together. Task functions, things that facilitate the job of the group so that it accomplishes its purpose, need to be made happen; relationship functions, things that promote good relationships between members of the group so that it maintains itself and does not dissolve, need also to be part of a group. And all of these functions, some of which we listed in the last chapter, are *leadership* functions. The tricky thing is that the fewer of them the designated leader finds himself or herself having to perform, the better leader he or she is. The best of leaders motivates the group members to supply these leadership functions—if not at first, at least in time. The best leader models the kind of behavior that he or she wants his or her followers to contribute, bringing them to group maturity.

Leadership is a *function* rather than a position. At any given moment a group member providing one or another of the task or relationship functions is performing a leadership function. To organize and define the roles of the members of the group, to explain or clarify what is expected of each member, to help develop an agenda and to help keep to it, and to suggest and help maintain channels of communication are all examples of task behavior. To be encouraging to other members of the group, to handle conflict in the group, and to share appropriate feelings with the group, whether good or bad feelings, so that they are not allowed to affect the work of the group are examples of relationship behaviors. The good leader may begin by having to supply most or all of these functions, but his or her goal is to motivate all members to share responsibility for them. One of Bart's problems, described at

the beginning of this chapter, was that he tried to use
the same style of leadership that was useful in an immature or beginning group in a group that was quite
mature and developed. He continued to supply everything when others were used to and wanted to contribute. They resented him and felt themselves unneeded. They lost interest.

Up until the middle of this present century, it was
thought that leadership used *either* task behavior or
relationship behavior; there were only two styles of
leadership, the directive and the non-directive or nurturing. We used to speak of the leader as either task
oriented or relationship oriented. Studies of the past
few decades, however, indicate that there are four
basic leadership styles, each one including some proportion of task and relationship functions:

High Relationship and Low Task	High Task and High Relationship
Low Task and Low Relationship	High Task and Low Relationship

High Relationship and Low Task style is a "coun-
try club" or social style. A great deal of attention is
given to the relationships between the members of the
group, lots of camaraderie, encouragement and relaxa-
tion. The work of the group is incidental and sporadic,
if there is any at all. Used in a work group that was
expected to be productive, such a style would usually

not be effective. Everyone might enjoy meeting for a while, but soon it would be apparent that "nothing is ever done." Expectations would be disappointed, since the group thought that they had come together to "do something." In such a group the purpose is not enjoyment first and foremost, although any group needs to satisfy to some extent the enjoyment needs of its members, but rather task fulfillment. The most supportive or encouraging environment cannot for long hide the fact that the group's main purpose is not being achieved.

This style, however, can be appropriate and effective in a group that has been, in the past, well developed and effective, but has hit a problem or situation that has stumped or demoralized them. It is a way of developing renewed loyalty, motivation and group cohesion. It can be productive in a group whose task, for the moment, is to build a team and renew self-confidence. It is also appropriate in a group where little attention has been paid to individual members in the past, whether due to previous strong task leadership or to pressures and the strain of the situation. Leadership is situational, so that each of these styles of leadership can be appropriate, given the right situation; no one of them is good or bad.

High Task and Low Relationship is a very directive style of leadership. Bart, at the beginning of this chapter, was good at this style and quite successful using it in the competitive world of business. It works well in a group that is developing or has lost its sense of purpose, a group that has no goals or criteria for success or that has become disorganized and meaningless. It is useful in many groups that are just beginning a group life with a need to have direction and purpose.

It provides some clarity of goals and purposes and offers close supervision over the implementation of these goals and purposes. It promises strength. It is appropriate in military and quasi-military groups.

It is inappropriate in a more mature group, a group that utilizes its resources well, knows its goals and purpose and successfully uses ways to achieve them. It was to this kind of a parish that Bart moved when he changed his headquarters. Without bad will on anyone's part, a mature group that has functioned successfully in the past might become offended by such "high handed" behavior of a designated leader; members might then simply lose interest, or they might redirect their energy to undermining the designated leadership, again without viciousness, because they are unaware of what is happening, as Bart was. In such a group, this style of leadership appears dictatorial; while intended as service, it is not seen as service. Such leadership can destroy a group, with the best of intentions. It is well rid of such leadership.

High Task and High Relationship is a style of leadership that is appropriate to use when first forming a group or community, and more appropriate and effective than the High Task and Low Relationship style for the beginning group. It calls for clarity of purpose and structures to attain it, as well as concern for nurturing good interpersonal relationships among the members of the group or community. Using this style, the leader cannot but model for the members the kind of behavior that will make the group effective and satisfying. As the members begin to perform some of the task and relationship functions, the leader is supportive of them; his or her aim is to develop the maturity of the group so that group members perform most of the leadership functions. His or her style of leadership and the service he or she supplies will change as the group changes.

It would be inappropriate to continue using this style of leadership after task and maintenance functions have been taken up by most of the members, since it would tend to destroy the growing maturity of the group and maintain their dependence on the leader, when dependence would keep them adolescent. A mature group would resent this type of leadership even more than they would resent the style of High Task and Low Relationship, perceiving, as they would, that their competence and talents are not being utilized properly and/or they are being "steamrollered." Their perceptions might go so far as to see such leadership as "phony." Used effectively and within limits, however, it can lead a group or community to the maturity whereby it can maintain itself effectively without a great deal of designated leader intervention.

Low Task and Low Relationship is a leadership style most effectively used with a mature group, a group that is clear on its goals and purpose, on structures that will help it to accomplish its aims, and knows how to maintain itself while pursuing its tasks. It is a catalytic type of leadership that would have been most effective in Bart's new parish. The decision to use this style depends largely on the past history of the group, whether it has shown competence in task and relationship functions in the past, whether it uses sound work structures, and whether it is attentive to the needs of its members. A directive style of leadership tends to aggravate such a mature group; it would rather use the talents of the leader in the same way it uses the talents of its members, capitalizing on his or her strengths and supporting his or her weaknesses. In this situation a leader might very well be primarily responsible for arranging for the physical needs of the group, meeting room, etc., preparing information that the group needs to know, acting as liaison for it and organizing its progress. His or her contribution of leadership functions will amount to supplying what others are not supplying. Most of all, as Stephen Clark has suggested in his *Building Christian Community*, his or her function might be to share with the community a vision worth making a reality, or, even better, helping the community to create its own vision. Clark calls this kind of leadership "environmental," having concern for task and relationship, but adding an element of vision that offers excitement and hope.

Used inappropriately with an immature community or group, a Low Task and Low Relationship style would be weak and unproductive. It would be perceived by the group members as "abdication," not giving the kind of strength and clarity that is needed for motivation. The immature community would feel leaderless, and well they would be, since no one is supplying the leadership functions needed! But it is a tribute to designated leadership when it can be used because he or she has led the group to greater maturity.

No one style is better than another; no one style is "good" or " bad." Leadership is situational and will depend upon the level of the community or group being led. Good leadership depends upon good judgment, the ability to judge the level of the group and to supply the most effective kind of leadership for that level.

Neither does a group always remain at the same level. A community that has experienced maturity could, for various reasons not all of its own doing, begin to regress to immaturity, becoming uncertain of itself and its direction. Leadership, then, needs to move from Low Task and Low Relationship to High Task and High Relationship, or, perhaps, to Low Task and High Relationship to build cohesion and community confidence. A parish council that once needed High Task and High Relationship may mature to the extent that this style becomes intruding, and the leadership style must change if it is to continue to be of service.

Life Cycle Theory of Leadership

Paul Hersey and Kenneth H. Blanchard have shared with us the results of their studies of leadership, and much of what is found in this chapter is my reflection on their basic work. (Cf. "So You Want To Know Your Leadership Style," *Training and Development Journal*, February 1974, pp. 22-37) They call their theory the "Life Cycle Theory of Leadership," a theory whose main value, it seems to me, is explaining to us how we can help a group or community to mature.

Group or community maturity may be described as the ability of members of the group or community to supply their own work structures, to achieve their goals, and to supply their own maintenance for interpersonal relationships. A mature group is one that appears to know what it is doing and why it is doing it, a group whose motivation is found in internal convictions. It is a community that is willing and able to take responsibility for itself, one whose members have the education and experience to accomplish its purpose. Age, of course, may affect the maturity level, but it is not directly related to the kind of maturity focused upon in the Life Cycle theory. In this theory, maturity is seen as psychological, not chronological.

Since followers determine whatever personal leadership power a leader may have, the leader needs to know what leadership functions the followers need to have supplied. As a group or community begins to mature, the leader best removes, very gradually, his or her task behavior; he or she allows group members to take more and more responsibility for work structures, on the assumption that members, now motivated internally, do not need to have external structures imposed. This process continues, presuming that the group grows in its success with task behavior, until the community or group is sufficiently self-motivated to allow the leader to reduce his or her relationship behavior. The more mature a group is, the less overt relationship behavior is required; it is not that friendship or closeness is less, but only that it need not be proven so frequently.

For example, if a leader wants to move a community from an immature level to a mature level of development, he or she best gives over to the group, and to individuals in the group, decisions about how they might best perform a particular task. If the individual and the group is successful in this effort, the leader reinforces their behavior with encouragement, support and positive feedback. Gradually the leader broadens the group's areas of task responsibility. And I emphasize *gradually*, since too quick a transference of such responsibility may be seen as weakness on the part of the leader, the group becoming demoralized from its lack of direction and failure to achieve its goals. This process continues until the group, community, or individuals are performing at a mature level, a level at which they do not have less task structure but rather at which their task structure is internalized. They should, then, be allowed to provide more and more of their own satisfaction for personal and emotional needs. The group is now motivated and reinforced in its accomplishment by the obvious trust the leader has in it, since he or she is no longer checking or supervising their every move.

An individual or a group may, of course, slip back from maturity to immaturity because of a personal crisis or new and strange work techniques or equipment. The leader, then, needs to increase task behavior, and perhaps relationship behavior, for the time, until the outside pressures on the group or individual have been resolved.

An effective leader needs to be able to use all four styles of leadership as they are appropriate. Weakness in one style or another needs to be acknowledged, allowing another to supply that style of leadership when the situation calls for it. The charism of leadership, it seems to me, is largely the ability to judge what style of leadership will be appropriate and effective in a particular situation. It is largely incarnational, calling for the development of human skills, the skills of observation, judgment and behavioral interpersonal relationships combined with knowing how to accomplish a task. No one is a born leader; we tend to use the styles of leadership to which we have been exposed and which we have found successful. But situations will arise in which those natural styles will be found wanting. We need to recognize those situations and develop new styles of leadership or allow others to use the style of leadership needed.

Jesus exercised a style of leadership that was effective for His purpose. He had a high task orientation, concerned about the accomplishment of His Father's work: "I have glorified You on earth and finished the work that You gave Me to do." (Jn. 17:4) He seemed driven to do His task: "As long as the day lasts I must carry out the work of the One who sent Me; the night will soon be here when no one can work." (Jn. 9:4) His exhortation to His followers was one of work: "Go, therefore, make disciples of all the nations." (Mt. 28:19) His message was of high relationships: "What I command you is to love one another." (Jn. 15:17) His style must have been highly relational, attracting, as it did, thousands of people. (Cf. Mt. 14:21) Such a style of high task and high relationships served the needs of a community not yet mature and just beginning to mature.

But Jesus also offered a vision, a belief of what life could be here in this world and hereafter. The vision seems also to be part of the charism of leadership: a final destiny of peace and good that a leader shares with his or her followers, or a destiny that he or she is able to help the followers to formulate. Such a vision was obvious in the leadership of John F. Kennedy and Martin Luther King; it was obvious in Peter, Paul and John XXIII. The vision required of leadership need not be religious, as the "Camelot" of the Kennedys witnesses to; but, it seems to me, for the Christian leader the vision must be rooted in the Person of Christ, His message and the Good News he preached: sin is forgiven, we are sons and daughters of God, we have been saved and need sin no more!

It would be dangerous to always follow the leadership style of Jesus, because our followers are not always of the same maturity level as the followers of Jesus. It would be equally dangerous to ignore the importance of sharing the vision of Jesus. The Christian leader needs a belief that is contagious, one that challenges the council, the parish, the community, the school, and the home to find their own vision in Jesus. There alone is our purpose for being a council, a parish, a community, a school, a home at all, if we call them Christian.

Christian leadership is like the Incarnation: it is human and divine. The human dimension of leadership is self-knowledge of the style of leadership I have already acquired and that seems to come naturally to me, and the development of those styles which I do not now have or feel uncomfortable with. It amounts to taking an inventory of skills I have and skills I need to acquire. Usually observations made by others on my leadership style are helpful in getting to know myself and my needs. It is difficult to diagnose our strengths and our needs alone. An instrument may also be used to diagnose our present skill level. Hersey and Blanchard offer one in the article referred to above. Many people I have dealt with have found this instrument useful. Once we know what we would like to learn, there is a need for practice, doing things we have not done before, or in ways we have not done them before. When I first began to learn different styles of leadership, for instance, I thought I was encouraging other members of my group with a very slight nod of the head. I learned that they did not "catch my message," so slight was the nod. But I wanted to learn how to be encouraging effectively. So I began to tell others when

I liked their ideas: "I like that idea" or "I like the way you express that." At first I felt simple, obvious, phony and awkward. Only with time and practice have I been able to make this particular leadership function a part of me.

The divine dimension of Christian leadership amounts, it seems to me, to the depth of my faith. The Christian leader will be religiously effective in proportion to his or her Christian optimism: the faith that we are already redeemed, that we need not sin, that this world is made to the image of Christ who has already triumphed. Our task is to remove the veil that hides His glory and the glory of the human world by using His message and the tools of His world. Such a vision is more likely to get a hearing today than one filled with cautions and fears, although, admittedly, there is much to caution about and fear. There was much to caution about and fear in the time of Jesus as well; yet, His Good News looked to joy and not to depression. The Christian leader needs the kind of hope born of an optimistic faith. He or she needs it because the Christian community needs such a vision.

The Life Cycle theory of leadership proposed by Hersey and Blanchard is valuable. The leader needs to be able to judge the maturity of the group before he or she can serve it. In addition, however, the leader has to share or help the group to surface a vision worth making a reality. For the Christian leader there is need to have a Christian vision.

Summary

A person may be a successful leader in one situation and utterly fail in another. Probably his or her success was luck: it happened that the style of leadership experienced and adopted was the style of leadership that the successful situation needed.

There are four styles of leadership, each one composed of some portion of task functions and some portion of relationship functions. Each style is most effective when used in the right situation. It is the responsibility of the leader to judge what is the "right situation." His or her judgment about the maturity of the group is crucial.

The leader can develop the maturity of the group by giving it, first, greater responsibility for task functions and work structures. When the group has assumed these successfully, he or she may then lessen relationship behavior so that the group may maintain itself. Throughout this process, the leader is regularly reinforcing maturing behavior with encouragement and supportive remarks.

The Christian leader needs, in addition, a Christian vision, either of his or her own or one arrived at through group work. It is this vision that identifies a Christian leader and community.

There is a need to reflect further on how the leader judges the level of a community's or group's maturity, to know what signs to look for and the indicators of maturity—in other words, what does maturity look like and what does immaturity look like? We shall explore these questions in the next chapter.

Chapter 3
Leadership: Reading the Group

The meeting ended with a good deal of confusion and hostility. Someone was heard to say, "I don't know if I can stand all this tension—I accepted this membership to help, but nobody can help with all this fighting!" The leader of the group, a newly elected Parish Council, was the most confused of all. This had been their third meeting, and it was not at all like the first two. Things had gone very smoothly during the first and second sessions, everyone was getting along, and people were at least polite to each other. But this time . . . !

As the third meeting had begun the agenda was shared and other items of business that might be added were elicited. The agenda had looked like this:

8:00 p.m.	Opening, Reading of Minutes
8:15 p.m.	Religious Education Parish Program
8:45 p.m.	Christmas Bazaar
9:15 p.m.	Report of the Ecumenical Committee
9:30 p.m.	Report of the Planning Committee
10:00 p.m.	Close

After the agenda was reviewed, the chairperson asked

if there were items of business that she had neglected
to include. Emil, a newly elected member of the Council, asked what kind of power or authority the Council
had; were they only advisory? The Constitution was
read, pointing out that, yes, the Council was advisory
to the pastor. Pat, also newly elected, suggested that
being advisory could place the Council in some very
frustrating positions, spending hours on work with no
guarantee that it would be taken seriously or even,
maybe, understood. Frank, into his second term on
the Council, pointed out that he had previously asked
that the Constitution be changed so that the Council
would be a legislative body, but no one seemed to have
heard him. Besides, maybe the Council needed to be
more attentive to parliamentary procedure and less
concerned with consensus. The discussion about the
Council being advisory or legislative and the use of
parliamentary procedure escalated from this point
until something of an uproar ensued, making it difficult
to pay attention to the work of the agenda. The chairperson suggested that the two issues be turned over to
a committee for study, and this satisfied Emil, Pat and
Frank to some extent, but by that time only forty minutes or so was left for business. The Religious Education Program description was handled indifferently,
leaving the Director of Religious Education to think
twice before she came to Council for help again, and
the Committee reports were given and received with
something less than enthusiasm. Emil, Pat and Frank,
the "trouble makers," left the meeting troubled themselves. The pastor had a feeling of "déjà vu": "It
seems to me I've heard this song before!" The chairperson wanted to quit. The Ladies Guild offered to
take over the Christmas Bazaar!

What To Look For

One group is not all that different from any other group, at least in the way it grows as a group. Its development is largely predictable. Our beleaguered chairperson might have saved herself a lot of soul searching and disturbance if she had been on the lookout for fairly predictable phases of group development. One theory, called Cog's Ladder, describes the phases of a group's growth by using the image of a five-step ladder.

The first step is the *Polite* stage, a time of ritual when members feel a need to be liked; it is time to become acquainted, to share some general interests, and to handle first impressions. Cliques might begin to form at this time, but they will become important only later. Conflict is unlikely in this phase. If there are hidden agendas, they generally remain hidden and do not affect behavior.

Rules of behavior in this first phase are to keep ideas simple, say acceptable things, and avoid controversy and serious topics—in general, to avoid disclosure and keep "masks" in place.

The second step is the *Why We're Here* stage, a time to try to define the purposes and goals of the group. Hidden agendas—that is, individual reasons for belonging to the group and plans for using the group—as well as cliques are most likely to begin to surface in this stage. Group identity is still low, since the importance of the group and its work is still foggy and individual benefits are still vague; expectations are uncertain. But the individual's need for approval becomes less, and more risks are taken than in the Polite stage. Even if the group's goals come from outside the group, imposed by others, there is still need for the group to discuss them, clarify them for themselves and adopt them as their own. Depending upon the task to be done, its length and its complexity, this stage may take more or less time.

The third step on Cog's Ladder is the *Bid for Power*, the stage that our innocent chairperson above discovered with shattering confusion! On the road to group maturity, members will try to influence the life of the group, and cliques will emerge quite visibly to employ the group for their own purposes. There will be efforts to influence the thinking of group members, striving for attention and recognition. Competition labels this stage. Leadership is at stake. Creative or novel ideas are often not acceptable, since they are seen as a bid for power, a demand for recognition of the individual's value to the group. In some groups, this stage can be as mild as a brief debate over the closing time of the session: Can it not be 9:30 P.M. rather than 10:00 P.M.? In other groups, such as our Parish Council described above, this stage can be sharp and destructive, at the very least preventing work from being accomplished. Some groups never get beyond this stage and do accomplish work, but it is generally of poor quality.

The word "Power" has taken on some degrading connotations through the years, but that should not lead us to believe that this third stage is a "bad" stage, to be avoided if possible. First of all, it isn't possible to avoid it if the group is to mature. It needs it as much as the child needs to go through a "negative" phase in which he tests his strength and autonomy; the child is filling a need to know what is his or hers. Individual group members need to feel they have some control over what they do and how they spend their time. They need to know they are not wasting their time or energies. This is the valid and legitimate source of the Bid for Power. Admittedly, it may get out of hand if not foreseen and handled properly, and we shall reflect on some ways to prepare for it and handle it constructively later in this chapter. All of this is said with an awareness that some members abuse this natural stage and use it to accomplish their less than praiseworthy ends! Even these, however, can be handled, often outside of group sessions, by the effective leader. As promised, we'll explore ways to handle such group problems later in this chapter.

The fourth step is the *Constructive* stage, the "team action" stage, characterized by attitudinal changes. There is more real listening to each other, more open-mindedness and acceptance of different value systems. Creative suggestions are welcome and fairly evaluated. Cliques largely disappear as a group identity builds. It is difficult at this stage to bring in new members, which explains why an effective Parish Council or Parish Committee becomes ineffective after the election of new members to its seats. The first three steps must be experienced by the new group until it is ready for this Constructive stage. Decisions or solutions reached in this stage, however, are often excellent and always readily implemented, since they are the decisions or solutions of all members of the group; each member, therefore, has a vested interest in their successful implementation. In this stage, talents and ideas of individuals are valued and used if given a good evaluation. Individual needs for recognition and satisfaction are met at the same time group needs are being met.

The fifth step on the Ladder is the *Esprit* stage, in which the members feel high group morale and intense group loyalty. Hidden agendas may still be present, but they do not affect group behavior adversely, either because members have granted to each other the right to have hidden agendas or because the trust level is high enough to satisfy the members so that no one in the group would misuse the group loyalty. There are emotional ties between the members, giving individual approval to members and allowing for individuality and creativity. The emotional ties are not possessive; there is a feeling of freedom since each member is in the group because he or she wants to be. It is in this stage that someone may suggest the need of a logo or identity symbol. In this stage the group is highly productive, accomplishing tasks beyond what the talents of the individual members would seem to justify. This phenomenon was called the "bonus effect" by the scientific teams of the National Aeronautical and Space Administration. The "bonus" is the superior product of the group and the personal satisfaction of its members. It is my experience that few groups reach this stage, while many groups pretend they do.

What To Do

As his or her group matures, the effective leader has less and less to do; initially, however, most of the functions necessary for group growth are his or hers—functions such as the task and relationship needs discussed in the previous chapters. These have a relative importance in each stage of growth.

In the *Polite* stage the leader needs to think

through what will be happening when the group first convenes: What is the place like in which they will meet, how are the seats arranged, is the lighting sufficient, etc.? The size of the group quickly influences how the seating can best be arranged; if it is small enough, a circle or semicircle seems to contribute most to encouraging the participation of all. Some refreshments, such as coffee, tea or soda, are useful to have as all arrive; in fact, they are more useful at this time than at a "break," since sharing refreshments together helps to ease any initial anxieties that participants may have. Friendly greetings by the leader and/or the leadership team also help. In short, the task of the leader in this first stage is to create a "climate" of psychological safety, an atmosphere of enough comfort to allay tensions that unnecessarily get in the way of people learning and working together. This may seem like "wasted time," but the effective leader knows that it pays off in the long run.

Once the session gets underway, there is a need for introductions; this can be done by each one individually, perhaps with the leader beginning so that he or she can model the kind of self-introduction that he or she wants; or members could be asked to pair off, learn something about another whom they don't know, and introduce each other. This latter approach is sometimes easier if members tend to be shy. I am sure that other elements sometimes go into this "climate set," such as creating ground rules for working together, eliciting the expectations members have of each other and of the group, etc., but these need to be thought through for each situation. The question the leader asks himself or herself is: "What needs to happen to put aside the dynamics that may get in the way of this group learning and working together?" There will always be some anxieties that members feel when they first convene, but they can be reduced to a healthy minimum. A healthy minimum allows those anxieties to remain that are necessary to challenge a group to work for a purpose. Too much comfort makes the group a social one in which nothing serious is expected to be done.

Another outcome of this introductory phase is to minimize the formation of cliques, self-supportive small groups that can be quite troublesome in the next two stages if permitted to solidify. Special efforts can be made to encourage those who came together to meet and begin to work with members they have not met. This can be done by "counting off" for small group work on expectations, for instance. The leader "counts off" one, two, three, four, five, six—each member accepting his or her number; the ones form one group, the twos form another, etc., until six groups are formed. Usually, those who arrive at a meeting together sit together; the "counting off" tends to separate them for work.

The purpose stage or *Why We're Here* stage usually is welcomed by the group as they begin to feel more at ease and curious or excited about entering upon a new venture. The leader is more task oriented in this phase, "getting down to business," as it were. His or her most important task is to share as much background information as possible with the group: how the need for it was first felt, the job that was envisaged, the hopes held for it, etc. Often, the leader can only be quite general at this point, since expectations and goals are necessarily vague at first, but he or she should make the effort to share his or her vision with the other members as clearly as he or she can. Sometimes I have heard a leader say at this point, "I suppose none of you are any clearer on why we're here than I am." This is not a healthy beginning!

Depending upon the history and nature of the group, as much freedom as possible should be given to it to formulate its own specific goals and objectives, within the framework, of course, of its general purpose for existence. In this way, members feel a vested commitment to the tasks of the group and are more likely to be motivated to do their part. This may be done by "brainstorming" needs that the group feels it may satisfy. Keeping in mind the general purpose of the group, all contribute the needs they see; these are written for all to see, but there is no judgment made on any of the suggestions at this time; it is a time of creativity, and we are not able to think evaluatively and creatively at the same time. When the members feel that there is nothing more to add, the ideas are evaluated, and goals and objectives are formulated for those needs chosen to work on. Accountabilities may then be assumed by members, one or more volunteering to be accountable for the objectives they would like to work on. Planning for the objectives then needs to begin, but I shall discuss techniques of planning later in chapter seven.

The third stage, the *Bid for Power*, may overlap the second stage, or it may not develop until the early stages of work or activity begin. The need for creating its own work structure may be quite strong in the group at this time. The leader needs, most of all, to supply the relationship functions at this time, with the hope that others will follow his or her example. Encouragement, harmonizing and compromising are "key." He or she needs to take seriously the ideas of the members, clarifying them and presenting them for total group discussion and decision. He or she may have to modify some of his or her own expectations at this time, an experience he or she will be comfortable with in proportion to his or her confidence in the use and effectiveness of group process. If he or she tends to feel comfort with a High Task style of leadership only, he or she will need to risk the use of Low Task and High Relationship. From experience, however, I am convinced that only after he or she has risked this a number of times and had some successes will he or she feel comfortable! His or her predisposition for McGregor's Theory X or Theory Y, as discussed in chapter one, is bound to be tested in this stage. He or she needs to be "cool" and courteous; he or she may also have to hold some things as non-negotiable, if they are imposed from outside the group or if, in his or her view, they are truly essential for effective group life. But he or she needs to take great care in labelling such essentials; group discussion may convince him or her that they are negotiable.

The "Bid for Power," of course, may only be tentative, testing the leader's own confidence and competence. If so, he or she can expect it to surface soon again. It may also be brief and inconsequential, such as changing the working time of the group. Or it may be quite serious, attempting to change radically the purpose of the group. Whatever form it takes, the leader needs to keep in mind that, more often than not, viciousness or evil intent is not a part of it; it is usually a normal stage of group development. That he or she does not become defensive is most important.

The fourth stage of group development, the *Con-*

structive stage, is enhanced by group exercises that highlight the value of cooperation, sharing, active listening, or team building in general. The leader begins to have a narrower range of responsibilities, since members have taken on some of the task and relationship functions. The leader can be most effective by asking constructive questions, summarizing and clarifying the thinking of the group, and allowing the group to come to its full potential by placing an obvious trust in it. He or she tries to blend with the others, being less directive and using more and more a Low Task Low Relationship style of leadership. He or she will be tolerant of the widely varying abilities of group members to contribute to the task of the group.

As mentioned in chapter two, a group may regress to any earlier stage of development for various reasons, internal or external to the group. The leader needs to be alert for such regression and change his or her style as a result. Again, it is the perception and judgment of the leader that makes him or her effective or ineffective. Arrival at the Constructive stage, therefore, does not permit the leader to lessen his or her sensitivity to group needs and maturity.

The final phase of group growth, the *Esprit* stage, makes few demands upon the leader while bestowing many rewards on him or her: the task and relationship functions are readily supplied by group members, group motivation is high, and work moves ahead with minimal support from the leader. The leader is rewarded with feelings of success and camaraderie. He or she still needs to be aware, however, of any signs of regression.

In this phase, the leader is largely responsible for the physical needs of the group, previous agendas, meeting place, time, materials, etc. He or she still needs to be readily available to the group, keep the relationships with other groups or authority healthy and continue an encouraging and supportive posture. But it is a beautiful experience and well worth all the preceding work!

Group maturity requires increasing support from group members as these stages progress: sometimes only one member needs to say "What's on the agenda?" to move the group from the *Polite* to the *Purpose* stage; the move from stage three, the *Bid for Power*, to the fourth, the *Constructive* stage, can be stopped by one strong, competitive group member or his or her clique; to move to *Esprit* calls for full group consensus. Hence, if a group is to grow, there is an increasing need for group cohesiveness.

When a Group Grows

So far I have spoken of the group in terms of a parish council, core group or committee. But what happens to leadership when the group becomes a system, an organization like Marriage Encounter, the parish or the diocese? All of the leadership skills explored above are still needed, but there are added complexities, most of which come from the increased numbers of individuals in the system, their need for communication and information, and their relative increased authority and responsibility.

Larry E. Greiner, while an Associate Professor of Organizational Behavior at the Harvard Business School, researched a theory on organizational leadership that is worth some reflection. He suggested that an organization went through five phases of development as it grew older and bigger.

Initially, there is a need for *creative leadership*, the kind of charismatic leadership that inspires the birth of a group and motivates it to action. The group is informal, enthusiastic about a new challenge, and characterized by regular communication and mutual support. The leader inspires more than directs. This phase comes to an end when confusion begins to characterize the group, a need for guidelines is felt and accountability seems lacking. A kind of malaise or indifference creeps into its ranks and the need of a stronger hand is evident.

To face this crisis of organization, a *directive leadership* is needed: a style of leadership that will establish procedures and channels, enforce definite regulations and call for regular accountability. The leader need not be charismatic; he or she needs to be an organizer. As the system continues to grow, however, this kind of strength is not enough. Members begin to feel stifled with rules and regulations; they complain about the lack of exciting creativity and begin to speak wistfully of the "good old days when the company (parish, church, diocese) wasn't afraid to take risks." In Greiner's language, the system has a crisis of autonomy on its hands. Members feel like robots, without control over their lives, or at least without control over what they do most of their lives: work.

The system then enters phase three; it needs a leadership that is comfortable with *delegation*. Appropriate members are given more responsibility, decision making is less centralized, and more discretion is permitted at the decentralized levels of the group. Communication still takes place from the "top," but it is more by exception than for direct management. Less uniformity is expected. Leadership is characterized by its responsible trust in the members of the system. Continued growth of the system, however, brings such leadership to feel that it has less and less control of the system; waste of personnel and materials may be suspected; unnecessary expenditures begin to appear. With the crisis of control, phase three begins to come to an end.

Phase four calls for greater *coordination* of the system's resources; it needs leadership that is able to conceptualize the total work of the group and coordinate its efforts. Overall, formal planning processes and review procedures are initiated. Resources are carefully allotted to the divisions that can best utilize them. Information on the state of the system is regularly collected centrally, but decision making remains untouched at the local level. If done well, all of these procedures aid the continued growth of the system until the procedures become more important than problem solving. This time Greiner calls the crisis one of "red tape."

Whereas the coordinative style of leadership relied on formal systems and procedures to accomplish the goals of the system, the *collaborative leadership* phase, phase five, relies more on interpersonal relationships and team work. "Red tape" becomes less as spontaneity is valued and the skill of handling personal differences is acquired. Problem solving through team action has priority; leadership seeks more to consult than direct decentralized areas or subgroups; educational efforts in team building and growth are made available, or even required, and rewards are given to teams more than to individuals. The leader in such a phase will have many of the characteristics of Michael

Maccoby's Gamesman. (Maccoby, Michael, *The Gamesman*, Simon and Shuster, N.Y., 1976) His measure of success is in the creation of winning teams. Greiner's study was not able to pinpoint the kind of crisis such leadership would generate, but his guess is that it would be around the psychological and physical stress placed upon the members of the group in their efforts to work with teams.

If Greiner's model rings true to you, as it does to me, you will see the wisdom of the leader who tries to diagnose the phase of his or her group or system. Each phase calls for some mixture of Task and Relationship functions, but, it seems to me, the proportions in each are different. The charismatic leader seems to have Relationship functions as a given, while the directive leader needs to work at them. Both the charismatic and directive leader are task oriented. The leadership of delegation calls for strong relationship functions with a minimum of task orientation, while the leader of coordination needs strong task orientation. The collaborative leader requires a strong belief in the value of interpersonal relationships.

Leadership requires this kind of judgment and the skill to use the style of leadership that the group or system needs. It needs to recognize that growth brings new problems that require a different kind of leadership. Only in death will time stand still and new problems not arise.

Summary

In this chapter we explored what to look for in a group and what to do about it when we found it. Without being deterministic, we can recognize that group growth is quite predictable. We can tell fairly well, with some solid information and careful thinking, where a group is now, where it has been and where it will be going (possibly) in the future. Such reflection tells the leader what the group needs *now*, and leadership is always in the *now*, not in the past or future; past needs have been handled and future needs have not yet arisen.

The small group moves through five possible stages: Polite, Purpose, Power, Constructive and Esprit. Each requires different kinds of things from the leader.

The system also has five phases: Creative, Directive, Delegative, Coordinative and Collaborative. Each requires a different leader, or different style of leadership.

I have no doubt that one leader can acquire the styles of leadership to give the small group what it needs in each of its stages. I am less certain that one leader can be equally comfortable leading in the five phases of system development. Notice, I did not say that one leader could not do it, only that he or she would probably not be comfortable leading in each of the five phases. In this light, the *situational* characteristic of leadership looms all the larger for me. Perhaps it does for you too, and, if so, now might be a good time to read chapter one, if you previously took my permission to skip it!

Whatever the stage or phase of a group or system, conflict is inevitable. The leader can use it for the good of all, or he or she can allow it to be destructive. In one way or another he or she handles it. In the next chapter I shall suggest some ways to make conflict beneficial to the group and the system.

Chapter 4
Leadership: Handling Conflict

A few days ago I saw a bumper sticker that read: "Christians are not perfect, just forgiven!" Christianity is a religion of reconciliation; Jesus handled and still handles the conflict between God and human beings well.

This is not to say that the Christian is a stranger to conflict. Conflict seems to make up the major part of our history. It was found in the earliest Christian communities: conflicts over the value of charismatic gifts (cf. 1 Cor. 14), over the place of women in the Church (cf. 1 Cor. 11:2-16), over leadership itself (cf. 1 Cor. 1:10-16). Nor need we look far for conflict in the Church today: conflict over the ordination of women, over a married clergy, over the preservation of the Tridentine Mass formulary, etc. The Christian leader, therefore, needs to know how to manage conflict; it is part of his or her community, as of every other community and group.

Our experience with conflict may lead us to bemoan it, to wish that it would go away or not arise at all. We may have found it usually to be destructive. Certainly, it can be, but it need not be. The danger of viewing all conflict as unwelcome is that our fear might

54

blind us to recognizing the usefulness of differences of opinion, the value of working through conflicting ideas to arrive at solutions or decisions that are more creative precisely because of the conflict. Differences, if not left unmanaged, can increase the group energy to work on a problem, heighten group innovativeness and actually lead to more effective problem solving. If they are unrecognized or left unmanaged, they will do none of these good things; they will stall the group or community, making for low productivity. We explored this a bit in the last chapter when we reflected on the "Bid for Power" stage of group development.

One theory of group dynamics, in fact, states that differences are useful for high productivity, provided they are managed. A group with few differences has little stimulation or possibility of creativity; a group with many differences that are not managed experiences clashes and disputes that also keep productivity low, if the group remains together at all. The ideal is for a group to have sufficient differences within it so that the end result of the group's work will be more creative than any single individual working alone would have produced. The trick is to manage the differences and the conflicts that arise from them.

One charismatic community I know of grew large enough a few years ago to consider splitting into two communities. Some members favored the split, while others did not, so that a conflict arose. The issue of ecumenical Holy Communion further complicated the conflict. Some members who did not favor a split felt that any Christian, Roman Catholic or not, should be welcome at the Communion table; others who felt a split would be beneficial thought that only Roman Catholics should be permitted to receive Holy Communion. Still other members held various shades of opinion on one or the other issue. The differences of opinion eventually brought the community to a crisis of survival, but its leadership fortunately knew how to manage conflict. It was decided to deal openly with both issues involved.

After a period of prayer, the leaders asked the members to form small groups in which all would be able to voice their views. They also furnished them with a process by which they might clearly define the real problem, look at some possible solutions, and settle on one to implement. All finally agreed on a course of action, supported it and contributed to its implementation. This particular group decided to split into two groups and to follow the policy of restricting the reception of Holy Communion to Roman Catholics, except in certain cases provided by Church law. In the process of making this decision and resolving their conflict, this group learned much about themselves, about the meaning of Christian community and about the value of conflict.

Competition —Cooperation

Competition heightens conflict. Participants perceive their goals as mutually exclusive: "If I win she'll lose; if she wins, I'll lose." Such an attitude is necessary if competitive sports, such as football, tennis or hockey, are to be fun. But goals are not necessarily mutually exclusive in all conflicts; in fact, conflict may arise where goals are not mutually exclusive, but they are perceived to be or assumed to be so, and a win-lose situation develops.

Such a complex psychological process is often at the root of conflicts that have no substantive cause other than the assumptions that one or other of the participants brings to the situation. If we approach another under the assumption that we are in conflict, we stereotype the other, perceiving him or her negatively and ourselves positively. Somehow this affects what we hear! We tend to hear and see only those things that we interpret as supporting our position; we filter out the things that do not support our view. Our mind registers these selected messages as reflective of reality and we behave accordingly in a win-lose way. Such behavior reinforces our assumption that we are in competition, so that we are involved in a kind of self-fulfilling prophecy. If the other person assumes a cooperative posture with us at first, it will not be long before he or she too becomes competitive. In fact, in a group where twenty-nine people are cooperative, if the thirtieth person is competitive, the group as a whole will soon become competitive among themselves. Most people do not like to lose.

Cooperation, the assumption of a win-win situation in which our goals are not mutually exclusive, allows us to manage conflict. Differences of opinion do not mean that we are not pursuing the same goals; we can still assume that "if you win I win and if I win you win!" Not every conflict can be handled as a win-win situation, because not every conflict allows all the goals involved to be achieved. What is important is that we examine the *reality* of the situation so that we do not labor under the fallacy that we are in a win-lose situation when it is truly a win-win situation. As we have seen, the acceptance of such a fallacy will soon change a win-win situation into a win-lose one.

The implications for the leader are important. Cooperative efforts are sometimes undermined by persons who view most activities as win-lose. The committee member who makes his or her living by selling, a competitive business in which win-lose is a valid assumption, may bring this attitude to every committee meeting. The leader needs to help create a climate of cooperation, to be prepared to intervene to prevent a win-lose response from triggering a competitive cycle that would subvert the cooperative venture, and to recognize that, while competition has its place, that place is rarely in problem solving groups or Christian communities.

We can bring the profiles of competition and cooperation into focus more clearly with the following comparisons:

Competition Win-Lose	Cooperation Win-Win
1. Behavior is appropriate in pursuing *own* goals.	1. Behavior is appropriate in pursuing goals *held in common*.
2. Secrecy.	2. Openness.
3. Accurate personal understanding of own needs, but *publicly disguised* or misrepresented: "Don't let them know what you really want most."	3. Accurate personal understanding of own needs and *accurate representation* of them.
4. Unpredictable, mixed strategies utilizing the element of *surprise*.	4. Predictable: while flexible behavior is appropriate, it is *not* designed to take others by *surprise*.
5. Threats and bluffs.	5. Threats and bluffs not used.

Competition Win-Lose	Cooperation Win-Win
6. Search behavior is devoted to finding ways of *appearing to become committed* to a position; logical, non-rational and irrational arguments alike may serve this purpose.	6. Search behavior is devoted to *finding solutions* to problems, utilizing logical and innovative processes.
7. Success is enhanced by forming *bad stereotypes* of the others, by ignoring the other's logic, and by increasing the level of hostility.	7. Success demands that *stereotypes be dropped.* Ideas are considered on their merit regardless of source, and hostility is not induced deliberately.
8. Takes extreme form when it is perceived that everything that impedes another from reaching his or her goal must facilitate reaching my goal. My goal is to *negate the achievements* of others.	8. Takes extreme form when it is perceived that whatever is good for others and group is good for self. *Will not take responsibility for self.*

Neither competition nor cooperation is good or bad; each is only appropriate or inappropriate. Effective group work, however, needs cooperation. In general, there is a need to keep sight of the goals and objectives of the group, maintain open communication, avoid "red flag" words, listen well, use task and relationship functions, and allow others to be wrong sometimes, come to their own conclusions, and change their minds without feeling like "sellouts." The leader can then use conflict for greater group productivity.

Conflict Resolution Strategies

There is more to handling conflict than assuming a win-win situation. As noted in the profile above, even cooperation can be overdone when one assumes that everything good for the group is good for oneself. We need to be responsible for ourselves and our needs even in cooperation. The leader, then, should be prepared to use strategies to resolve conflicts that allow for individual needs as well as group needs to be met.

Conflict can be *avoided*. The leaders of the charismatic community described at the beginning of this chapter tried this strategy at first. They hoped that if the problem was ignored it would go away. Sometimes such an approach to conflict is successful, particularly if the issues involved are not serious or are obviously arising from self-interest that can be identified and counseled privately. More often, however, as in the case of this community, to avoid the fact of conflict allows it to grow more serious and extensive. Members are given time to form firm opinions without the sound information that a conflict resolution process offers. They become committed to private solutions without giving themselves time to look at the real problem.

Conflict can be *defused*. When the leaders of this community did begin to acknowledge the conflict, they delayed acting for its resolution. Defusion usually is a way of allowing things to cool down so that the issues can be discussed more rationally. It can be useful, and, at times, even necessary. It may take the form of trying to resolve minor points while avoiding the major issues, or it may actively keep the issues so unclear that there seems to be no way of handling them.

Usually, in the end, however, both avoidance and defusion lead to crisis, as they did in the community discussed above. Conflict that is not managed generates that distrust that is the greatest enemy of community: bad feelings, suspicions and misunderstandings run rampant. When the conflict does surface, it is often destructive. It seems to me that it is the leader's responsibility to facilitate the surfacing of the conflict in a constructive way, using the differences as an occasion of learning for all and of greater productivity for the group. He or she does this, I believe, by using a process of reconciliation.

Conflict can be *reconciled*. Fortunately, this is largely what the leaders of the above community finally did. Reconciliation of conflict is a process using four basic skills: diagnosis, initiation, listening and problem solving.

Diagnosis searches out the type of conflict that is presenting itself. A conflict of values, such as that surrounding the reception of Holy Communion by non-Roman Catholics, is the most difficult kind to resolve. In the case of our community, it was resolved on the basis of Church discipline. Those who held that the Eucharist was not only a sign of unity but also a means to unity could still retain this value while recognizing the need for obedience. But Church discipline or doctrine is not always available. A "real" or tangible conflict is easier to handle, such as the question of splitting the community. Since values are not usually involved in a "real" conflict, compromise is easier to attain. If the leader, especially, is to avoid confusing himself or herself and others, it is important to diagnose the type of conflict that needs to be resolved. Such diagnosis requires collecting all of the appropriate information, becoming informed of "givens," such as the constitution of the group, state, city or church laws, knowing the human dimensions of the conflict, such as previous or incidental hostility between members, etc.

Initiation is the skill of taking the first steps toward reconciliation: when and how to approach the persons or group involved. Sometimes it is best done by sharing with the others the effect that the conflict is having upon oneself: "Whenever I sense conflict among us, I get upset and just can't concentrate on our work." At other times, the leader may have to acknowledge that there is a problem that the group needs to face. Little is gained by attacking: "Look what you are doing to each other!" and much can be lost in this way. The members may become defensive and hostile, creating a new problem without solving the previous one. The leader needs to sense that the conflict is serious enough to call for group handling, that the group can handle it and that it is now ready to do so. He or she should be prepared with a process through which the group can work out the conflict.

Listening is the skill of hearing another's point of view, the ability to understand what is being said verbally as well as non-verbally. If the leader hears what he or she does not want to hear, he or she may be tempted to respond with a "hard line" or in a threatening fashion. This will probably not further his or her efforts toward reconciliation. Especially in the initial phases of conflict resolution, all the parties need to be reflective, clarifying and paraphrasing what the other is saying, so that both perceive that they are understood and understanding. There is a great need at this stage to assume a win-win situation and not to allow any stereotyping to filter our hearing. When both sides feel satisfied that an accurate understanding of their view of the conflict has been grasped, other factors may be presented, but always in a non-judgmental fashion. This often leads to the lowering of defenses and to increased appreciation of other elements in the issue that were, perhaps, not before considered.

Problem solving is a process for reconciliation, as well as a skill. It is more structured than the skills of diagnosis, initiation and listening, involving, in this model at least, three distinct steps. There are, of course, many other models, but this seems to me, from experience, to contain the best of most other models. Some prefer to call this a model of decision making as well as problem solving.

The first, and most important, step is to define the problem. Too often we neglect to take the time to do this and begin to develop solutions for what seems to be the problem. We are surprised a week or a month later when the same conflict seems to be still with us, but why should we be? After all, in not taking the time to agree on the real problem, we have solved a problem, but not the real one! In every problem there are a hundred problems. We need to take the time as a group to decide what the basic problem seems to be, so that we can solve that. In this stage, we share with each other what the problem seems to be at first glance, without working for any consensus. Having shared that much, we immediately move on to the underlying factors of the problem. Only when we have exhausted these do we move ahead to attempt to define the problem and come to a consensus on it. This is best done in small groups at first, so that all members are encouraged to contribute. When each group has arrived at agreement, the various definitions of the problem are shared with all and the large group works toward a common consensus.

All return to their small groups for the next step, the brainstorming of possible solutions to the problem as agreed upon. This is the creative phase of the total process, so it is best if no evaluations of the contributions are made until members have nothing more to contribute. Even "wild" ideas are acceptable in this step, the theory being that some of the best solutions come from "wild" ideas that are modified and polished. This step is usually fun if we are able to tap into the creative flow of the members.

The third and final step of the process is the evaluation and decision making phase. The "pros" and the "cons" of each of the suggested solutions from step two are looked at and discussed. Some of the solutions may be combined, but eventually two or three possible solutions are agreed upon as workable and as promising success. From these one is chosen for implementation.

A word of caution. This process of conflict resolution presumes that participants perform many of the task and relationship functions described in our first two chapters. All need to be ready to be supportive, to share appropriate information, to help to regulate the discussion so that the group remains faithful to the process, and to be able to harmonize and compromise when it is needed. Without the members feeling committed to these responsibilities, the leader's efforts to resolve conflict by utilizing all of the members' talents can be an agonizing experience.

The value of the process is the speed with which the solution is implemented, since all have contributed to its formulation and share a vested interest in its success. One-sided resolution of conflict can reach a solution more quickly, but its implementation is delayed by the necessity of persuading others to "go along." The use of "power" to resolve conflict is rarely effective, often creating more conflict than it resolves.

This method of discerning the Spirit is fully incarnational. It calls for the leader to learn very human skills and to appreciate the very human way in which men and women work. At first its use will feel awkward and unnatural, like an artificial tool that hinders more than helps, but perseverance is well rewarded. Besides helping to solve problems and resolve conflicts, it also helps to build community. It is one way that the community can be reconciled to itself, and, being one in mind and heart, it is one way to make visible the unity for which Christ prayed: "May they all be one. Father, may they be one in us, as You are in Me and I am in You, so that the world may believe it was You who sent Me." (Jn. 17:21) And, after all, to lead us to such unity is the task of Christian leadership.

Confrontation

The initiation step of the conflict resolution model described above sometimes involves confrontation, whether one on one, one on group, or group on group. In addition, there are instances when confrontation alone might be effective in the handling of conflict, without using the conflict resolution process. Unfortunately, confrontation carries with it some unpleasant overtones. Understood properly by the parties involved, however, it can be seen as a truly caring activity; in fact, after speaking on confrontation on one occasion, I had a woman approach me and say, "You know, every time you used 'confrontation' I thought of '*care*frontation,' because if you don't care about others, you don't take the time or make the effort to confront them!" I knew the theory, but I had never thought of it in such beautifully tender terms.

Confrontation takes place when one person (the confronter), either deliberately or inadvertently, does something that causes or directs another person (the confrontee) to reflect on, examine, question or change some aspect of his or her behavior. (Cf. Robert R. Kurtz and John E. Jones, "Confrontation: Types, Conditions and Outcomes," *The 1973 Annual Handbook for Group Facilitators*, University Associates, pp. 135-138) It may be to point out some discrepancy between what the confrontee says and what he or she does, to highlight resources that the confrontee seems not to be aware of, to focus on a confrontee's weakness, to correct or fill in gaps in his or her information, or to encourage him or her to action. Note that it always involves behavior, not motivations or intentions, and that it may be a pleasant experience when we are able to open the eyes of the confrontee to strengths or virtues which he or she did not know that he or she possessed. Confrontation is not always around negatives!

All that we said about initiation above applies to confrontation, but there is more. Our wording seems to be most important for the success of our confrontation; it is well to state first the confrontee's behavior that is the cause of concern, then its effect upon me and its consequences for me: "When you so quickly put aside my suggestion, I feel dumb and useless, and I'm unwilling to try to contribute again," or "When you helped me to think through my suggestion today, I felt important and helpful, and I'm looking forward to our working together." The formula might be stated: confrontee's *behavior* + its *effect* on me + the consequences for me = C where C = confrontation, or

$$B + E + Cons = C$$

Obviously, each of us must do our own confronting; I cannot confront for you since my expression of your feelings and the consequences for you are not credible fully unless they come from you. The leader, certainly, needs this skill, but so also do the group members.

For successful confrontation, it is helpful if certain conditions are present:

Conditions for the Confronter:

1. Has a good relationship with the confrontee or, at least, is aware of the quality of his or her relationship.
2. Accepts the confrontee and is willing to become more involved with him or her as a person.
3. Phrases his or her confrontation as a suggestion, rather than a demand.
4. Directs his or her confrontation toward concrete, specific behavior that the confrontee can recall, rather than to motives.
5. Makes his or her confrontation positive and constructive, rather than negative.
6. States his or her confrontation briefly and directly.
7. Represents facts as facts, hypotheses as hypotheses, and feelings as feelings.

Conditions for the Confrontee:

1. Accepts the confrontation as an invitation to explore himself or herself.
2. Is open to know how he or she is experienced by others.
3. Is willing to tolerate some necessary, personal disorganization which may result from the confrontation.
4. Responds differently to different modes of confrontation, rather than responding in a stereotyped way, i.e., accepting all confrontations as truth, or dismissing all of them as worthless.
5. Hears and understands what is being said to him or her, reflects on it or asks for clarification without becoming defensive, such as "Well, the reason I did that was. . . ."

Group Conditions:

1. If confrontation takes place in a group, there should be a fairly high level of trust and acceptance in the group.
2. The confrontation should fit the goals of the group; confrontation within a faculty meeting or at a social gathering, for instance, could be quite disruptive, since it is not within the expectations of such groups.

Since no one can tell beforehand the effect that confrontation will have on the confrontee, it is well to elicit from him or her some "feedback" on what impact it had. Otherwise, wounds might be opened without need and long range effects can be painful.

The confronter needs to know his or her own

motives for making the confrontation, for not all confrontations are done out of altruistic reasons; he or she needs to avoid taking out his or her frustrations on a weaker group member with confrontation, to avoid using confrontation to ward off possible confrontations of himself or herself by others, etc. Some questions the confronter might ask himself or herself before he or she begins to confront are: (1) What is the purpose of the meeting or group? (2) What is the psychological state of the person I am thinking of confronting? (3) What are my motives? (4) Am I confronting another's behavior or motives?

Summary

For the skillful leader the management of conflict can be a very satisfying experience: the trust level of the group usually rises after it has worked as a team to resolve a conflict; chances are that the work level will also be higher and more enthusiastic. Perhaps the resolution of conflict requires the leader to know himself or herself better than any of his or her other functions require: his or her motives, commitments and assumptions about people. Certainly, whether he or she is habitually cooperative or competitive will have a bearing on his or her style.

The resolution of group conflict is often a combination of good confrontation and problem solving. It is likely that the earlier the conflict is dealt with, the less damage it can do and the speedier its resolution. But conflict resolution takes time; the cost of not taking the time may be the disintegration of the group or system, so it is worth the time if the group or the system is important. The conflict resolution process offered in this chapter takes less time as a group becomes more familiar with it; such familiarity will, no doubt, aid the group to work on any group problem in a better and more satisfying way.

Even the Christian leader needs the skill of confrontation, for he or she is no greater than the Master who came to "bring fire to the earth" (Lk. 12:49) by confronting the secure and the powerful. He has taught us that confrontation is not easy, but it can be saving!

Confrontation is a kind of "feedback," which I shall explore with you in the next chapter. The better we know how others experience us, the better leaders we can become.

Chapter 5
Improving   Our   Leadership
Style

The corporal wanted his child to be a general! "I met a man," said the corporal as he grew loquacious, "and he told a great thing; he said we can make of babies what we will! He said, 'Come, you tell the baby often enough what you want him to do, and when he grows up he will do that.' Over and over I would tell this baby, 'You will be a general.' Do you think it will be so?" (John Steinbeck, *Tortilla Flats*, Modern Library, N.Y., 1937, p. 179)

We don't know whether the baby became a general; my guess is that he did, because I tend to believe the "great thing" the man said. Much of our lives is strongly influenced by what others have told us about who we are or what we should do. Grown-ups forget how scary it is to be a child, to be dependent for everything in a strange, new and, above all, big, strong world. We latched on to any message that would help us to find our place, be identified and play our role with security. Our style of leadership is not immune to this subtle persuasion. Most of us learned what we know of leadership from watching others and listening to their advice. What school offers a degree in leadership, or even requires courses in it? Chances are, then, that we learned how to be a leader by chance. And we may be good at it. Or we may find ourselves too frequently ducking it or failing it. The point is that leadership is a learned skill, and I believe that most of us can learn to do a passable and satisfying job at it. We may have to unlearn a few things and learn new ones, but most of us can do it with strong enough motivation. And if you are one of those frequent members of the Church who find yourself surprised to be thrust into a leadership position, that should be motivation enough. Who wants to be embarrassed?

The Johari Window

Recall from our first chapter that leadership is not leadership unless it is so perceived *by others*. To be effective, the leader needs to know how others see him or her. "Feedback" is the jargon name we give to this process of learning how others see us. Some say it is like looking into a mirror, but that is not fully accurate, since we see in a mirror only what we can see ourselves. Feedback is more than a mirror; feedback is a verbal or non-verbal communication to a person or to a group, providing them with information either (1) about how their behavior is affecting you, or (2) about how your behavior is affecting them, or (3) about your here-and-now feelings in self-disclosure fashion. The word "feedback" comes to us from the field of electrical engineering, where a rocket, for example, has a mechanism that sends back messages to the ground indicating whether it is on or off target. The ground mechanism then corrects the course if necessary. Since we cannot "see ourselves as others see us" unless they tell us, we ask for "feedback" to determine whether they see us as "on course" or not.

Speaking with a physician who holds a leadership position in one charismatic community, I learned of the importance of feedback for the leader. He spoke of the value of feedback sessions among the leaders of the community, perceiving such sessions as a way to personal growth and a way of visibly caring for each other. What I remember best about his discussion with me was his thought: "Feedback is always a little painful, so it must be a 'lot gentle.' " I agree.

One way of making things gentle for me is to know the rationale for what I am experiencing, the theory that says this experience is useful for me. The Johari Window is the name of one theory indicating the value of feedback; its name comes from its originators, *Jo*seph Luft and *Har*ry Ingham. The Window is made up of four panes, and it looks like this:

ARENA	BLIND SPOT
FACADE	UNKNOWN

The Arena is a clear pane of glass through which I can look at myself and others can look at me; therefore, it contains things I know about myself and others know as well.

The Blind Spot is a one-sided glass, since others see things in me, but I cannot see them myself. Their view is clear glass, while mine is frosted.

The Facade is also one-sided, but turned the opposite way: there are things about myself I see clearly, but others can't see, perhaps because I don't want them to see. My view is clear glass, while theirs is frosted.

The Unknown is a frosted pane of glass for myself as well as for others; there are things about myself that I do not know nor do others know.

When trust in a group or with another is high enough, we can widen the Arena pane and lessen the space for the Facade by sharing our feelings, perceptions, anxieties and hope that we have been hiding. When we have that kind of trust, we can solicit feedback from the others, particularly for us leaders on our leadership style, and widen the Arena further while lessening the area for the Blind Spot pane. Feedback may even lessen the area of the Unknown by surfacing earlier assumptions or experiences that are reflected in our present behavior without our previous awareness. Probably, however, since it is unlikely that we shall ever know ourselves entirely in this world, something of the Unknown will always remain. Through feedback our Window could look like this:

ARENA	BL. SP.
FACADE	UNK.

This suggests that most of our activity in the group is straight and above board. Hence, there is less likelihood that others will have to make guesses about us, with the accompanying danger of misinterpretation and consequent misunderstanding. Such openness may not be appropriate with casual acquaintances, but it has been found helpful in community, committees and working groups. It is helpful wherever interpersonal relationships are significant for the goals to be achieved. It is most helpful for personal growth and development.

The leader can also use this model better to understand group members. The member who is regularly soliciting information from the group with questions like "What do you think of this?" or "How do you feel about what I just said?" while never sharing what he or she feels or thinks is probably maintaining a large area of Facade and may be pictured like this:

ARENA	BL. SP.
FACADE	UNK.

In time he will probably evoke reactions like "Hey, you always want to know how we feel or think, but we never know where you stand!" He'll or she'll probably cause irritation, distrust and withholding.

The opposite of this kind of group member interacts with the group by giving a great deal of feedback, but eliciting little: "It seems to me that we are just wasting time again. Why can't we stick to the subject?" or "I really like to work with this group; I get so many new ideas!" He or she never solicits feedback. If he or she receives it, he or she does not seem to understand it, or he or she reacts in a way that discourages any further attempts at feedback from the others, i.e., he or she gets very angry, cries or leaves. He or she is unaware of how he or she is perceived by others, and, as a result, many of his or her attempts at self-disclosure seem out of touch, evasive or distorted. He or she continues to behave dysfunctionally, since he or she does not have the corrective help of feedback. His or her profile looks like this:

ARENA	BLIND SPOT
	UNK.
FAC.	

Another type of group member that the Johari Window helps to understand is the person who does not say much about himself or herself, nor does the group know much about him or her. He or she is more an observer than a participant. His or her profile looks something like this:

Ar.	Blind Spot
Facade	Unknown

Such an individual uses a great deal of energy in maintaining himself or herself as a closed system, so that there is little left for productive group work.

The Johari Window is useful in two ways: (1) it gives the leader a rationale for the usefulness of feedback sessions with other leaders in the group, as well as an appreciation for feedback on himself or herself from group members; (2) it helps him or her to understand better the consistent behavior of dysfunctional group members, so that if he or she feels it useful to confront them, he or she has a scaffolding from which to work or even share.

The Quality of Feedback

Feedback, whether I give it or receive it, has certain qualities that enhance its value for learning.

Feedback always focuses on behavior. Only the individual knows what he or she intended by his or her behavior. Others can know his or her intentions only if he or she shares those intentions with them. But there is no way of hiding my behavior, and it is to this that others respond. Their feedback on my behavior can help me to examine the congruence between my intentions and my behavior, so that I may choose to maintain my behavior or to change it. The person always has this freedom if feedback is given properly: we may choose to use it or not. For that reason we need not be afraid of feedback; the final choice of its value is up to us. Of course, there are certain consequences of choosing not to change behavior that is ineffective, incongruent with my intentions or bothersome to others. But the fact is that we are free to accept these consequences. Good feedback does not remove our freedom. It is always given in a way that the other can *hear* it, *understand* it without distortion, and *choose* to use it or not.

Feedback is best when it is specific. A leader in a community might be told, "John, I really like you and I find your leadership effective in many instances. But I wish you would share more of the responsibility and tasks with others. We want to do something too." Such a perception might be very helpful to John, but it would be even more helpful to point out individual instances where John did not share sufficiently: "John, I really like you and I find your leadership effective in many instances. I'd like to reflect with you on how you worked to find a meeting place for us. Do you remember how you did it?" It is important at this time to recall accurately the behavior of the one receiving feedback. It is important that he or she can recall it himself or herself, since we learn little from what others "say" we did but cannot remember. Once the behavior has been recalled we can move on. If it is not recalled it is best to drop the topic as diplomatically as possible. If we do succeed in jogging the memory, however, we continue: "Yes, that's what I recall also. How did you feel at that time?" It is sometimes helpful to encourage John to get in touch with his feelings. We can then share with him the effect his behavior had on our own feelings and explore with him how he might have behaved differently or the value of repeating his behavior in the future.

Feedback is non-evaluative. Let's suppose John has said, "I did all the searching for our meeting place myself because I really didn't feel anyone else wanted to do it, or could do it." Evaluative feedback would respond, "That's arrogant and stupid. Do you think you are the only one interested in this community?" And so might begin an unproductive uproar. Evaluative feedback may attack the self-esteem of the person, frequently making him or her defensive and non-responsive. Then the problem only becomes escalated. My response to John, on the other hand, could have been non-evaluative: "John, when you say that, I feel degraded and incompetent, so that I'm not sure this community needs my talents." My tone, of course, needs also to be non-judgmental; if said in anger or exasperation, even this response could be evaluative. If said in a factual way, however, it does not judge John as a "good" or a "bad" person. It simply shares with John the effect of his behavior on me and encourages him to take a look at it. But we reflected on this to some extent in our last chapter.

Feedback in a group is most valuable. It is possible for John to answer my admission of feelings of being degraded by saying, "I don't think you should feel that way," and if I am alone with him there is little I can do without becoming defensive. In a group, however, I could then ask if anyone else felt as I did. If others support such feelings, it is most difficult for John to defend his behavior, no matter how good his intentions were. Again, John could reject such feedback, but he should ruminate on the effects of his behavior before doing so. At any rate, he is given the opportunity to understand the feedback objectively, the effect of his behavior on others, rather than an opportunity to hassle with a single individual. This presumes, as explored above, that there is an environment of trust and acceptance in the group and that such feedback does not violate the expectations of group members.

Feedback is most effective if it is immediate. What is of significance to one person might well go unnoticed by another, so that if too much time elapses between the behavior and feedback on it, the response to the feedback might well be, "I don't remember doing that." Without recall, feedback has hardly any constructive value. If a core group or leadership group does not meet frequently enough, therefore, the opportunity for feedback is lessened. Each might receive feedback on its behavior in the core or leadership group meeting, but behavior of some weeks ago would probably not be material for feedback. Ideally, a group that feels comfortable with feedback might set aside the last fifteen minutes of each meeting for a group self-evaluation. This is particularly useful in the Activity phase of group development.

The receiver has a responsibility for effective feedback. Since a feedback session is a learning session, the learner shares responsibility for learning with those offering feedback. Defensiveness or rigidity hinders learning. Given properly, feedback should be heard and understood by the receiver. He or she does best not to respond immediately, but to make sure that what is being said is being understood without distortion. They might ask questions to clarify what they are hearing, even repeating it substantially out loud, or inwardly in their minds, so that they can later settle on its value and whether to act on it or not. The value of feedback is almost always lost if the receiver immediately responds with a reason for his or her behavior or a statement of his or her intentions: "I certainly wasn't acting out of hostility!" The same is true if the group finds itself being drawn into a long, intellectual discussion of the feedback.

Feedback has wide implications for the Christian leader. Since leadership is leadership only when perceived as such by others, it is the single, most valuable way of learning how others perceive him or her. As a Christian, it is one more indication that we take the Incarnation seriously. We accept the revealed truth that we become what God calls us to be in community. Feedback is a human tool for deepening the trust and mutual respect of the community. To recognize its value is to accept our humanity, to use, as Jesus did, the things of this world to save this world. For Christians, I believe, there is nothing that they can put aside as "only human"; otherwise, I would not be putting my time and effort into this book. All things are created and maintained in Christ: "For in Him were created all things in heaven and on earth. . . . He holds all things in unity." (Col. 1:16a & 17b) The Christian leader may be charismatic; he or she is a man or woman of faith; he or she is most certainly human. Belief does not make us less human.

Some reflection on the Blessed Trinity leads me to believe that God is in a constant state of feedback! As the image of the Father, the Son is feeding back to the Father who He is; He is the on-going reflection of the Father: "To have seen Me is to have seen the Father." (Jn. 14:9b) In the Son the Father always sees Himself. In the Father the Son sees Himself. The Spirit is the emanation of this on-going feedback, the love of the Father for the Son and of the Son for the Father. Love is also the ultimate goal of feedback for us. It is, at the same time, where feedback begins. This should be no surprise to us, for, after all, in whose image are we created?

The examples I have used in this section may lead the reader to think that feedback is only negative, sharing with another only his or her dysfunctional behavior. But this is certainly not true of "feedback" within the Blessed Trinity. Feedback is positive also, pointing out helpful behavior in another that should be repeated. As discussed in chapter 2, by using positive feedback a leader can bring a group to greater maturity. With God, as with us, positive feedback is a beautiful experience.

Hidden Agendas

In any group or system the members have aspirations, attitudes and values, not all of which they need to, nor should they, share with other members. Each member joins a group to fulfill or express some personal need, and that is quite legitimate. St. Thomas Aquinas expressed it by saying that our will responds only to what seems good to us; God made us that way. We may join a group to fill our need for belonging, acceptance or recognition, needs that Abraham Maslow found were quite normal and healthy. Such needs are not "selfish" nor "of the flesh" (sarx), as St. Paul describes that which is not of the "spirit." (Cf. Rom. 7:5) Only when the needs of one member block another member of the group from fulfilling legitimate needs is there need for concern. As we reflected above in chapter 3, there may be hidden agendas even in the Esprit stage of group development that are acceptable. Hidden agendas are found in the Facade or Unknown areas of the Johari Window; they are reasons for behavior that we are unwilling to share openly with others or that not even we are aware of.

Should the leader suspect that there are hidden agendas that are obstacles to the goal fulfillment of the group, he or she may, without indicting the legitimate need of the individual to fulfill himself or herself, do a number of things, in addition to confrontation.

He or she may help to surface unhealthy hidden agendas near the close of a discussion by saying, "I wonder if we have explored all that we need to on this issue. Maybe we might just go around the room and ask individuals for comments that might open up further thoughts." This is particularly necessary to do when he or she suspects that the consensus he or she has is only a false consensus in which silence is taken for consent.

The leader should not criticize the group for suspected hidden agendas, for this would only rigidify obstacles. Neither should every hidden agenda be dealt with in the group; some can be handled outside the group on an individual basis. Often it is enough if people know they are understood and being heard.

The leader can facilitate the surfacing of obstructive hidden agendas by allowing the members to have a large say in the creation of an agenda and in how the group will work together. This has its best opportunity in the Purpose phase of group development and in how the leader handles the Bid for Power phase.

Summary

The leader is not expected to be a mind reader, but he or she needs to know how others are perceiving him or her, the rest of the group and the task that has to be done. And most people do not want to take the risk of revealing all of this immediately, nor can they, since the group, the style of the leader or the tasks are not yet clearly identified as a group convenes. Perceptions take form slowly as group life grows.

The Johari Window is a useful cognitive tool for understanding the known and unknown areas of group life. It is a rationale for understanding the value of feedback.

Effective feedback is a community building tool, heightening the levels of trust and acceptance. Because it deals with our self-image, it is an art; used improperly, it is a weapon of considerable strength. The leader needs to know the art, and fear the weapon. As a Christian, he or she is called to hammer "swords into ploughshares," to make a death-dealing instrument into a life-giving tool of growth. (Is. 2:4)

The leader need not know everything about every member, although the highly skilled leader might be almost able to do just that. Members, including himself or herself, have a right to privacy. His or her concern is the health and vitality of the group, and not all unknowns or hidden agendas threaten these.

Every group needs to make decisions; in fact, how the group does this has considerable bearing on its health and vitality, its morale and self-image. How to make decisions, therefore, is of concern to leadership; for that reason, we turn to this topic in our next chapter.

Chapter 6
Leadership and Decision Making

Communal discerning of the Spirit calls for vision, sensitivity and prayer. It presumes, ordinarily, that the community has opened itself to the Spirit. It requires that the community, as well as individuals, be able to distinguish between its own voice and that of the Spirit. It may require time. Still, it is the single most significant criterion upon which decisions in a Christian community are judged. Christian decisions are expected to reflect the manner of Christ, who said, "I may be testifying on My own behalf, but My Father who sent Me is My witness too." (Jn. 8:18)

Leadership in the community needs to be sensitive to the Spirit if it is to help the decision making of the community. Because the community is human as well as spiritual, leadership needs also to serve the community by being skilled in some of the human dimensions of group decision making. Where the human dimension is ignored or considered unworthy of consideration or felt unneeded, the Spirit may find it most difficult to be heard. For this reason, we shall now consider some of the human dimensions of community or group decision making, ways that decisions are made, the basic qualities or characteristics of decisions, a process for decision making, and reasons why groups flounder about in indecision.

The Second Vatican Council's *Dogmatic Constitution on Divine Revelation* underscored the importance of community insights and decision making to make God's Word relevant to each day and age. Speaking of our Christian faith, it stated: "This tradition which comes from the apostles develops in the Church with the help of the Holy Spirit. For there is growth in the understanding of the realities and the words which have been handed down. This happens through the contemplation and study made by believers . . . through the intimate understanding of spiritual things they experience, and through the preaching of those who have received through episcopal succession the sure gift of truth." (par. 8) The teaching from bishops and priests and deacons is *one* way to discern the Spirit; the decision of a believing community is another. And both are subordinate to the Word of God. (*Ibid.*, par. 10)

The leader can facilitate sharing of "the intimate understanding of spiritual things" which he or she and the community members experience, as well as the sharing of the results of their contemplation and study, by being skilled in some communal decision making processes. Where the community finds it must make a decision in which they know the Spirit should be involved, the first task of the leader is to clear the way for the voice of the Spirit by helping to create an atmosphere in which individuals feel free to express their ideas and insights, an atmosphere of ready and sincere exchange where trust and mutual acceptance thrive, an atmosphere in which the shy are encouraged and the overly aggressive are tamed without being crushed. The leader who is effective facilitates a *private* as well as a public commitment to the group decision.

The use of the task and relationship functions discussed in chapters 1 and 2 will help him or her to assure both of these outcomes. In addition, he or she will find it valuable to reflect on how decisions are made in his or her community. Decisions are being made all the time in a community, often without the leader or the members themselves fully realizing it. A parish picnic may be planned because a men's or women's group has always sponsored a picnic. How was it decided to continue this tradition? It has been decided to build a church proper in a parish that has been using an all-purpose hall for liturgical celebration. How was that decision made? It is decided that the parish budget is to be reviewed by the parish council. How was that decision reached?

Ways Decisions Are Made

Any individual may attempt to make a decision for the group. If he or she receives *no* support from other members, he or she has laid a "plop." There has been no sharing of ideas or insights, it is not a decision that only authority or an expert can make, and both publicly and privately it is clear that his or her decision has been rejected. As for the individual who regularly "plops," receiving no acknowledgement from other members, he or she will eventually make fewer and fewer contributions until he or she withdraws completely, feeling that his or her talents are not appreciated.

Sometimes a member may feel that he or she has the *authorization* to make a decision for everyone. He or she may assume self-authorization because he or she does not value the insights or ideas of others. Or he or she may feel himself or herself to be, and truly be, the only person with the information necessary to make the decision. Sharing of insights has been minimal; he or she may or may not abandon his or her self-authorization when it is clear that most of the members do not support his or her decision. This type of decision making is a tempting trap for the leader who does not share information with others or who assumes that his or her position in the community gives him or her the prerogative to decide for others on all occasions. The latter assumption may be true, as supported by some theologies of Church authority, but that does not make this leadership style much more effective. Usually, leaders, even in the Church community outside of the hierarchy, are delegated by the community to make *some* decisions on their own, and it is best if they are clear about such expectations and autonomy. The community reserves significant decisions to itself, decisions about what members can expect of one another, about how community information is shared, and about how decisions are to be reached. Individuals forming the community may delegate authority, but they cannot delegate their proper responsibility; in fact, no one can delegate responsibility.

A third way decisions are made is by *handclasping*. An individual makes a decisive sounding suggestion and another member or two support him or her, giving the impression that there is general support for the decision. For one reason or another, other members do not intervene, even if they disagree or don't like the suggestion. Consequently, others feel trapped into being committed to a decision they do not favor, or they feel frustrated and unneeded. The group can become stagnated and indifferent.

Conflict and pressure become more overt when a *minority* tries to decide for all. The minority publicly and privately embrace the decision, sharing their resources and talents freely. Some of the majority might even go along publicly with the decision, but privately they reveal that they really don't agree with it. They remain, for the most part, uncommitted and non-participative. Implementation of the decision is most difficult if more than the minority are needed to make it a reality, since others have no vested interest in the decision.

Voting allows the *majority* to "win," which indicates that there are some losers. In itself, voting assumes a win-lose, competitive situation, which does not offer the best environment for community growth. Usually, however, there is greater commitment and utilization of resources when decisions are made by the majority, the minority often going along publicly. Actually, the minority often has low enthusiasm for the decision and its members do not commit their talents to its implementation to the fullest. They feel like "losers" who have been "steamrollered." They therefore may feel competitive, waiting for their turn to "get back," or may grow increasingly indifferent. Admittedly, voting may be the only way of reaching a decision when consensus seems unlikely because of the size of the group or because of radically different value structures in the group. It is probably better to decide with a vote than to stand still!

Consensus is usually the healthiest way for the group or community to make decisions. It is reached by the whole group, even if this has to begin with small group discussions reaching decisions that must then be reconciled by the whole community. It is done best in groups small enough for all to be heard. It is not possible in a group where radically different value structures are found, such as in politics. In coming to consensus, individuals do not agree for the sake of agreeing, for such commitment would be short lived. They agree because they truly see something of value in another's position, or at least in part of another's view. Compromise and harmonizing are central functions for consensus. All are expected to speak from reason, even though they might have strong feelings on the issue; irrational, emotional, defensive arguments are not expected. Still, emotional reactions are understood and tolerated, and managed! It is the search for reason and truth that eventually touches all with its validity. It seems to be a viable way for making decisions in the Christian community, since all are presumed to share the same radical values and norms as rooted in the Word of God.

Consensus can be *false* if it is reached by taking silence for consent. The leader needs to obtain some sign of agreement, verbal or non-verbal, from all members; it may look like a nod of the head or an enthusiastic statement of agreement. If the leader suspects the consensus to be false, it is time to go around the room member by member to elicit the thinking of each one on the decision. Often this will open the issue up all over and consume more time, but it is better than having members express non-support outside of the session.

It is *forced* if external pressures, i.e., external to the individual or group, seem to require a commitment to the decision. Members might "go along" because there is "nothing else we can do," but the implementation of the decision will be long in coming, unless that, too, is forced. At any rate, members may never see the decision as "theirs," so that it will not be effective in the long run.

True consensus permits all to express their ideas without feeling threatened or too readily judged. Cooperation is crucial for such consensus: "If you win, I win; if I win, you win!" Differences of opinion are seen as enriching, not as obstacles. Decisions from true consensus are quickly and enthusiastically implemented. The group that reaches true consensus is often at the threshold of the Esprit phase of group development, if not already in the door.

To get a better comparative view of these ways of making decisions, reflect on the chart on p. 92, based on an imaginary group of ten persons.

"Good" and "Correct" Decisions

One Parish Council I know of made a decision to build a gym. It seemed like a "good" and "correct" decision, the parish being somewhat remote from the city and its facilities for youngsters. A parish gym would "keep the kids off the streets." So a fund raising drive was initiated. The drive failed, and after two years the idea was abandoned!

There could be many reasons for such failure, but in this case there seemed to be a main one: the initial decision was made by "handclasp" and was railroaded

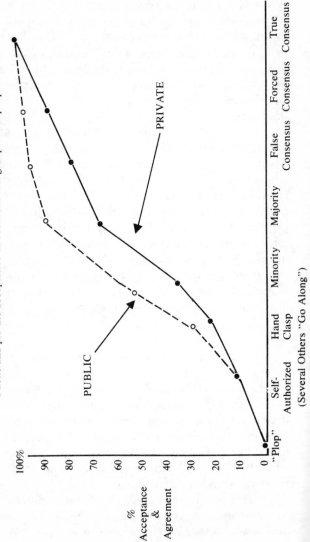

HOW DECISIONS ARE MADE

Public and private acceptance of decisions in a group of ten people

PRIVATE

PUBLIC

| True Consensus | Forced Consensus | False Consensus | Majority | Minority | Hand Clasp | Self-Authorized (Several Others "Go Along") | "Plop" |

100%
90
80
70
60
50
40
30
20
10
0

% Acceptance & Agreement

through. The pastor, a former director of youth in the diocese, was deeply committed to the youth ministry, even to the extent that he instructed the president and treasurer of the Council to see that such a resolution for a gym "got passed." They succeeded in getting the decision made, but they failed to get it accepted for its successful implementation.

We are sometimes deluded into thinking that there is such a thing as a universal or "best" solution to a problem, led on, as we are, by the advice to "get the facts, weigh and consider them, then decide." We then assume that there is a single right solution or decision to be reached. This is sound thinking and advice for decisions that do not involve people, for decisions in matters of technology. In such decisions, we may assume that, if things don't work out, it was due to some oversight and we need more information. Hence, we may collect information and formulate plans for the reunion of all Christian Churches for years, attempting to improve our solution to the problem of disunity, while the fault may lie elsewhere! It is possible that any number of plans for unity might work if Christians themselves supported them. As soon as people are involved in a decision, feelings, attitudes and opinions impose a second dimension on decision making.

The first dimension of a decision is its "quality." The quality of a decision concerns whether it is objectively the best or the poorest way to accomplish our purpose. The second dimension is its "acceptance" level, the degree to which members are committed to its implementation, believe in it and are satisfied with it. Where people are involved, the most excellent of decisions may be ineffective; effectiveness depends upon acceptance.

Let's reflect on our rural parish discussed above.

Plans for a better youth ministry that might have been developed might have been many: plan A, plan B, and plan C. Perhaps plan A was by far the best. Yet, in this particular parish, with this kind of population, it is very conceivable that plan B would have been the most effective, although not of the highest quality. Naturally, the degrees of difference between the "best" and the "poorest," as well as the consequences of each decision, need to be studied. The fact remains, however, that an inferior plan or decision might be the best for getting results, if it has acceptance and support. This may be the reason that Frank Lloyd Wright said, "A camel is a horse put together by a committee." It tells us that if we want to act with support and effectiveness, we may need to be content with less than highest quality decisions. Like it or not, we do—sometimes.

Quality requires wisdom, understood as the product of intelligence and knowledge. Acceptance requires satisfaction, the product of involvement in decision making. The method for achieving one is not always the method for achieving the other. There is no one best approach to decision making. The approach is often indicated by the very nature of the problem to be solved or the decision to be reached. We explored one way of problem solving when we discussed conflict resolution in chapter 4; we shall shortly explore another, but similar, method in this chapter. But, in fact, there are hundreds of methods for making decisions, especially for making group decisions. The ones we offer in this book have, in my mind, the best elements of the hundreds, but they too have their limitations.

Problems are different; decisions are of different kinds. They require different processes or approaches. When a decision does not touch the lives of other people and it requires an immediate solution, such as whether to call the fire department when our house is on fire, group decision making would be inappropriate, a waste of time and, perhaps, disastrous. Such decisions do not require people satisfaction or people involvement. We do not need to worry about acceptance, again, if we can implement the decisions ourselves successfully, such as whether to cut the grass or do some reading—unless, of course, others are affected, such as if another is trying to nap while we cut the grass outside his or her window! In short, there are times when we are free to make a quality decision without concerning ourselves with the acceptance dimension of decision making.

Most of us in church leadership positions (or most leadership positions in groups or organizations) do have to be concerned about acceptance. Perhaps, for our effective decision making, acceptance is more important than quality. Parish or prayer group decisions need the support of their people. To decide to build a gym or to split our charismatic group touches the lives of the members; such decisions require their acceptance if they are to be successfully implemented.

A quality of leadership is to be able to analyze a problem or a decision in terms of its objective, quality or acceptance. It is difficult to have both all the time, but we can have some of each all the time.

A Way of Decision Making

If only quality is required of a decision, leave the decision to the expert or experts. If acceptance is also needed, the persons affected by the problem should participate in its solution. Before a session of group decision making, members should be supplied as much relevant information as possible. At the beginning of the session they should spend some time on how they will work together, what they can expect of each other and the leadership, and how decisions will be reached, e.g., whether by vote or true consensus. Also, there is always a temptation to jump to quick solutions, without first agreeing fully on the issue or the problem; some may be assuming that a quality decision is best and, therefore, the goal of the group, while others assume that while the group will strive for quality, acceptance is the prime target. Opening up discussion on these areas is not a waste of time, since, if we do not spend time on them in the beginning, we shall probably have to spend time on them later. The leader needs to be sensitive to the task and maintenance or relationship functions, to group development, and to underlying assumptions of win-lose that can landmine a group. He or she needs to be careful not to dominate the group, especially if his or her position is rather prestigious in their eyes; without intending it, the group itself can invite his or her domination by making the leader the "answer man" or "answer woman," asking question after question of the leader with all dialogue traveling between the leader and the group, rather than among group members themselves. If the leader dominates, the decision reached will be his or her own, and he or she might as well have made it by himself or herself.

I have found it best if the leader is prepared to offer a decision making structure to the group. One such structure was discussed as part of the conflict resolution exploration. Another is a six-step process as follows.

Identification of objective(s). The group asks itself the question, "What are we really trying to accomplish?" It may be that there is more than one answer to this question. If so, the group has to choose its prior objective at this time. It is important that the objective be realistic, within the power of the group to achieve.

Identify obstacles and problems blocking the achievement of the objective. A single problem often includes several other problems or obstacles; list these separately for all to see. A great deal of time need not be spent on these first two steps, if all feel free to contribute and can agree in general on the elements or parameters around which they are in need of a decision.

Select the issue or problem whose solution seems to have the greatest potential for allowing the group to move toward their objective. The objective is the criteria upon which the group bases its decision at this point. It is helpful if the objective is written out fully where all can see it. This step may be somewhat time consuming, since it calls for consensus. It is, in fact, a crucial step, since the rest of the process and time will be given over to making a decision about *this* issue and not the others. If even one member does not agree at this point, he or she will become more and more resistant as the process continues, eventually stating something such as: "Well, I never thought this was the real problem in the first place!" This can be so frustrating to group members that they don't want to experience it again, so they stay away from group sessions. As a result, their resource is lost and the long term survival of the group may even be threatened. Thus this step is worth the time given over to it. The group may decide to "call it a night" after this step so that they can resume work on the issue at the next session. It is an acceptable time to take a break before continuing.

All possible alternative decisions are generated. The group responds to the question, "What are all the possible decisions that could be made around this issue?" Using a brainstorming technique, as described in chapter 4, the group thinks creatively about the issue. All suggestions are written down for all to see. It is important that no evaluation take place at this time. The only restriction to keep in mind is that it is a decision about the agreed upon issue that is being brainstormed, not one of the other issues put aside for the moment.

Evaluate all the possible decisions suggested in the brainstorming. The main criterion for evaluation, of course, is the statement of the issue agreed upon in step 3: "Does this solution or decision handle this issue?" Other criteria may also be developed, such as cost, timing, valuable side-effects, undesirable side-effects, resource limitations, and potential acceptance by others beyond the decision making group. Assess the potential consequences of each decision or group of decisions if grouping seems called for; weigh the forces that would help the decision to be implemented against the forces that would oppose its implementation.

Finally, choose a decision and plan for its implementation. This step, like the third step, requires consensus if *all* the resources of the group are to be marshalled for its effective implementation. Sometimes the planning required is extensive, and therefore I shall share some planning structures with you in the next chapter; at other times, the planning may be quite simple, a case of deciding who will convey the decision, how it will be given, to whom it will be given, etc.

Some Reasons for Group Indecision

If a group gets stuck in its decision making process, it can do several things: run over the elements of the problem in rapid succession several times to see if some pattern emerges, switch the representation system from abstract to concrete terms or from verbal to graphic or numerical representation, go back to the starting point, or simply take a break. Sometimes these techniques unblock the process and the group can make progress.

Sometimes they do not, and it is helpful if the group or organization leader knows some of the reasons decisions are not made. This is by no means an exhaustive list.

Individuals and/or subgroups within the group are paralyzed with fear of the consequences of any decision at all. They cannot act because they are taken up with a concern about what "those in authority," not part of the group, will think or say, or what the public might think if a decision were to change some aspect of their image before others.

Another reason for indecision is that group members belong to groups other than the decision making group. Loyalties may be divided, operating as hidden agendas that stymie or pressure behaviors of various kinds. Such loyalties may make members indecisive one time and impulsive another, forming their opinions without really thinking through all the dimensions of the decision being discussed.

Split loyalties may become more severe when they occasion interpersonal or interfactional conflict, still another reason why groups sometimes cannot make decisions. Defeating another, or defending oneself, becomes more important psychologically than hearing and weighing the contributions of others. Such members hear selectively what they expect to hear, as described in our discussion on win-lose situations; they judge the value of ideas more on personalities than on their own merits.

A fourth reason for group indecision is that they are frozen into one way for making decisions, such as *Robert's Rules of Order*. But, earlier in this chapter, we reflected that different decisions, issues or problems often call for different approaches or structures. The leader, especially, needs to make a continual effort so that the group is not frozen into one method for making decisions, since no one method is appropriate or helpful for every decision to be made.

A fifth reason for indecision we have already alluded to in step 3 of the decision making process suggested above in this chapter: lack of clarity in stating the problem. The director of one management seminar states: "This phase is extremely important, deserving lavish (where necessary) expenditures of time and effort in order to both identify the problem, refine it, and through this process secure member internalization and commitment to it. Groups frequently are foredoomed to failure, even tragedy, when they inadequately clarify the nature of the problem." (author unknown, unpublished seminar paper, "Decision-Making Processes in Groups.")

I also discussed above in this chapter something of the sixth reason why groups cannot come to decisions: there is premature testing of alternatives or making of choices. Our natural instinct upon hearing a proposal is often to evaluate it, and more often to evaluate it negatively. Yet, ideas are fragile creations, shriveling up when met with a chilly or indifferent reception. To evaluate idea by idea as they arise does not create the kind of supportive climate that · could encourage idea production and the pooling of a wide assortment of ideas before the important task of evaluation is undertaken.

Certainly, there are many more reasons why groups become or remain indecisive. These are only a few. The implication for the leader is that he becomes more effective as he becomes a better diagnostician. He needs to know the roadblocks his group faces, and it is also helpful if he knows what is going on with those who place them, either deliberately or unintentionally. The six reasons given are only meant to stimulate the leader's own diagnostic skill.

Summary

The more I think about it, the more convinced I am that a central skill for the leader is decision making—not that he or she makes decisions (although he or she must do that too), but that he or she knows how to help his or her group or system make decisions well. In this chapter, we saw that there are healthy and unhealthy ways to make group decisions and that decisions themselves are beset by the crossroads of "quality" and "acceptance." A process for group decision making was explained and some reasons for indecision were suggested.

None of this suggests, of course, that the prophetic office no longer exists in the Christian community. God chooses His own prophets, for "the wind blows wherever it pleases." (Jn. 3:8a) One person may direct a community with a vision that is truly of the Spirit; his or her decisions may be those of the Spirit. But the true prophet is a rare breed. Ordinarily, the community must come to its decisions by way of the Incarnation, using all of the human skills and techniques that help groups to rally around a chosen direction. It is to this ordinary, normal requirement that paragraph eight of the *Dogmatic Constitution on Divine Revelation* refers, as quoted above.

The history of God's interventions into our world has followed a pattern. He reveals Himself to an individual, such as Abraham or Moses. He changes them in some way and shares with them a message of significance, but of significance for others as well as themselves. He gives them a message for a community, whether it be the community of mankind, as in the case of Abraham, or the community of Israel, as in the case of Moses. In Jesus He revealed Himself for the Church. In each case, the message is preserved and safeguarded by the community, so that it may make the message relevant for each generation.

On occasion, God sends His prophet to bestir the community and to prod it to a truer interpretation of His message, but, more often than not, He leaves the community to use its created talents and its gift of the Spirit to decide upon His will.

Chapter 7
Leadership and Planning

Once the decision is reached, it is time for planning. If the decision is an enthusiastic group decision, plans for its implementation may be equally enthusiastic—and haphazard! They may take such general form as: "Jack, will your committee be responsible for the publicity? And Mary, will you find the materials and people we need to help present the program?" Once accountabilities have been accepted, everyone might feel that the planning is complete. What has really happened is that the program has been dumped in the laps of the few; they are sent off to sea with wishes of luck or offers of help if needed. If things work out, the few are sometimes congratulated; if not, they are always accused, in private if not publicly.

But planning is as much a group responsibility as decision making, although requiring a different process and set of skills. The whole group may not be expected to work out the nitty-gritty details of every step, but it is expected to be responsible for the implementation of its decision. If accountabilities are accepted, they are accepted in a cooperative way; the group still remains responsible for the carrying out of the decision. If the accountability is successfully accomplished, the group is expected to learn what made it successful in cooperative review of the task; if it is not successful, the group searches out what not to do again! Review or reporting of accountability is not a time for blaming or praise, but a time for learning.

Planning is hard, patient work. Just as we want to jump to the solution in decision making before we identify the problem, we want to jump to the accomplished goal in planning before we look at the steps necessary to get there. One poet has said, "The fault of the age is a mad endeavor to leap to the heights that were made to climb." (Ella Wheeler Wilcox) Usually, the courageous stories that are directed to motivating business and industry do not do the same for those of us involved in the Christian ministry. One such example is: "Consider the planning done by Captain Gabe Bryce, former pilot in the Kings Flight, who took the 122-foot-long Vanguard airliner off its 1,260 yard runway for the first time and guided it through the only gap in the encircling hills. For two years he rehearsed every move, did his finger exercises in the cockpit of the prototype every day, invented emergencies and met them." If you are like me, I am not sure what kind of exercises I do to plan a parish program of adult education or to plan a successful fund raising project. I understand what Gabe Bryce is intended to teach me: that I must plan very carefully. I also understand that my way of planning needs to be quite different from his. In this chapter I shall share with you some methods of planning I have found successful in Christian ministry.

A Planning Process

A working definition of planning: forward thinking about courses of action with a full understanding of all the factors involved, and directed to specific, measur-

able objectives. The first temptation to be overcome is
that we cannot measure the success or failure of meeting our objectives, since we are a spiritual organization. Still, Jesus Himself said we could: "Make a tree
sound and its fruit will be sound; make a tree rotten
and its fruit will be rotten. For the tree can be told by
its fruit." (Mt. 12:33) That we are believers does not
dispense from the need we have to be accountable, to
be able to determine by the accomplishment of our
objectives whether we are succeeding or failing, and
why. The alternative is to live without learning, to
have one year's experience fifty times, rather than fifty
years of experience. Below I shall suggest ways of
measuring even spiritual objectives. I agree that we
shall not know the full impact of our spiritual work
until Judgment Day, but we need not spend the time
between then and now repeating mistakes.

   Identification of needs is the first step in planning.
We need to determine what need our goal and objective will be meeting. We need to know whether the
need we identify falls within our area of responsibility,
our organization's reason for existence, our purpose.
The purpose for which we exist is the umbrella under
which we are gathered, the reason this group is together. In the light of our purpose, we can brainstorm
needs we see that require attention if we are to fulfill
our purposes. Facts about people, the community, the
parish, the prayer group, and the Church need to be
surfaced: what are the concerns of the people, where
are they in their life together, what have they expressed an interest in, what is needed that may not be
in the awareness of everybody but of which more
could be made aware? These are the kinds of things
going on in the heads of the groups as they brainstorm
"needs."

When all needs within the purpose of the group have been expressed and noted for all to see, they are *collated and analyzed*. Similarities and trends are noted and underlying factors are searched out until the group is able to settle upon a specific set of needs to which it agrees to address itself. If the group is very large, this part of the process, like the next, may be done in small groups of no more than eight persons a group. However, it is not impossible to complete this step with as large a group as two hundred working together, provided that the leader or facilitator is quite capable.

When the needs have been agreed upon and written down for all to see, there is an opportunity for private prayer or reflection if the group is so inclined. Following such a time of prayer and reflection, other needs may be surfaced, discussed and, through consensus, added to the list—or some of the previously agreed upon needs may be deleted in the same way. At any rate, a final list is accepted for the *formulation of goals*. A goal is a positive statement, usually beginning with "To," whose accomplishment will fill the need expressed. It is usually a general statement, such as "To increase the participation of minority group persons in community affairs," or "To assist the aged persons in the community to find comfort and enjoyment in their lives." It may be as much as a five year goal, but never so futuristic as not to have an influence on present action. A goal could be a one year goal, but usually it is broader than that. I have found success with five year goals that can be revised each year if circumstances so suggest. Another group, for instance, might have undertaken or accomplished one of the group's goals, so that it no longer need be pursued, or the situation may have changed in the past year so as to make the goal of a year ago undesirable. The important thing about a goal is that it be based on a true need.

When the group is satisfied with a set of goals whose fulfillment would help them achieve their purpose for existence, *objectives are set*. An objective is more specific than a goal, and it is always measurable. It is a task that needs to be done as a step toward the achievement of the goal. A goal could conceivably have one objective, but usually it has several. An objective might be: "To help twenty percent of the heads of households from minority groups to become employed." It is a task to be done within this working year. Another objective might be: "To employ five members of minority groups in our school system this year." From this phase of the planning process the name of "Management by Objectives" comes. It is a phase that is preferably done by the entire group, but I have also had success with a committee formulating objectives for the goals agreed upon by the whole group, and then offering these objectives to the whole group for their acceptance, modification or rejection.

The nitty-gritty of planning begins once the objectives are agreed upon. For each objective, one or more members of the group have to be accountable by name. They are to see that the objective moves toward completion, making regular reports on progress or problems to the group or to a subgroup designated by the group. These persons need to formulate the program or steps they will follow to implement the objective, the criteria upon which they will judge themselves successful, the resources of people and/or material they foresee to be needed, perhaps the costs of such resources, and how and to whom they will report progress and completion of the objective. I have found it more effective if developing such a detailed plan was done by the people accountable, and only then presented to the whole group for their acceptance. Objective sheets would have the following categories:

Goal Statement:
Objective Statement:
Accountability:
  Program: 1.
               2.
               3.
         etc. as necessary
Criteria of Success:
               e.g., Fifty people will attend adult
                     education programs
                          and/or
                     Eighty percent of the people
                     attending the program rate it
                     valuable
Resources: People   Cost
               1.
               2.
               etc.
               Material   Cost
Reporting:
               e.g., Bimonthly progress reports to
                     the Parish Council
                     Final report in writing to the
                     executive committee by June
                     15, 1978

Planning takes time, but it also saves time. It saves the time of frustration and directionless action, the ennui and disinterest time, that usually occurs without planning. It saves the energy of the group from being splintered into a multitude of different directions that lead to no common purpose or set of goals.

Planning requires work, but perhaps no member benefits more from it than the leader. If done properly, and it will be after a little practice, it leaves the leader with a blueprint of expectations, what is expected of him or her, and what he or she can expect of others. It can motivate the group as they regularly follow their progress in what they set out to do. It can be a tool for on-going learning as analysis of the objectives and their progress reveals facets that the group had not thought of in their planning. In other words, the time and work put into planning will be used anyway, but without all of the benefits that come from planning.

Planning for Change

The kind of planning we have just discussed is somewhat elaborate, done probably once a year. There is another methodology, called the "Force Field Analysis," that is useful even more frequently; it can be used also in conjunction with planning by objectives, especially as the nitty-gritty task of planning out each objective emerges.

Force Field Analysis, as the name implies, involves predicting and analyzing the factors that will help the objective to be implemented and the factors that will be likely to oppose its implementation. Planning always involves some kind of change; we want to move from point "A" to point "B" and that is a change. The Force Field Analysis, based in the field of physics by the physicist and human relations expert,

Kurt Lewin, postulates that for every driving force for change there is a resisting force. When we analyze the forces in our field of change, we construct a picture of what it will look like as we try to make our objective a reality.

Every situation or "status quo" is composed of driving and restraining forces that maintain the present situation. When the sum of the forces driving for change equal the sum of the forces resisting change, a situation is stable. When they become unequal, because there is a change in the strength of one or another, a change in one or the other force's direction, an addition or withdrawal of a force, the situation becomes unstable and change occurs.

To illustrate, take a simple committee meeting. As the meeting convenes, all the possible forces are poised, but not yet active. Should the leader increase his or her own driving force by strong task orientation, pointing to the clock or reprimanding people who chat, it is likely that restraining forces will increase as well: people will feel hurt and participate less, bringing the task no closer to completion. On the other hand, should the leader allow chatting and the exchange of trivialities indefinitely, he or she would be decreasing the restraining forces with the result that tensions would lessen. Still, the group might not accomplish its task, since too little time would be given to it. The trick is to do both at the same time.

The leader recognizes that people need time to chat and be heard at the start of a session; there is a human need to phase into a new situation or task, need to give time to let go of where we have been. The leader handles this need with relationship functions and, thereby, decreases potential restraining forces, such as preoccupation with personal needs that get in the way of listening. With task functions, the leader increases the driving forces for change, moving the group toward the accomplishment of its task. Members retain their freedom while moving as a unit toward their objective. The leader analyzes the meeting, the situation, in the light of chapters 1 and 2 and, knowing the things he or she has going for him or her and those he or she has against him or her, he or she is attentive to both, lessening his or her opposition and strengthening his or her support. With this analysis he or she enters the meeting, behaves appropriately with relationship and task functions and moves the group to its objective: he or she has planned for change.

Force Field Analysis is a "cognitive map," a mental structure that guides us in analyzing what to expect and how to handle it in any planning or change effort. We can outline our projections on a sheet of paper. The "status quo" or the present situation is a line down the middle of the sheet. At the top of the sheet is written our objective. To the left of the center line we list the forces we have going for us to meet our objective, the "driving forces": the people who will be supportive and helpful, the material resources we have available, the program we have developed to meet our objective, the methods we intend to use to make our program a success, the priorities of those who will be affected by the change. There may be several other factors we feel we can count on. To the right of the center line we list those factors that we foresee resisting our efforts to implement our objective, the "restraining forces": the people who will be resistive, their priorities, their resources, etc. Another program to accomplish what we seek might have already been tried and failed, or there might be alternative programs that compete with ours. These should be listed among the restraining forces.

Upon completion we have before our eyes a picture of what we have undertaken: the "field of battle" as it were.

The next step requires some rather incisive thinking. Assigning a hundred points to each side of the line, a hundred points to all the driving forces and a hundred points to all the restraining forces, we distribute them according to the strength of each of the forces. The strongest supportive force on the left side of the line might be judged to be worth forty points; the strongest restraining force might be judged to be thirty points. The weakest driving force might be only five points strong, while the weakest resisting force might be worth ten points. Other forces on each side might be judged to be worth twenty or thirty points in power. The end result of our estimations is the sum of one hundred points on the left and one hundred points on the right. Now we have analyzed not only *what* forces we need to work with, but their *relative strength*.

I have always found it useful to make such estimations together with those who have first-hand information about the forces involved. If this cannot be done, then at least our "guesses" should be checked out with such a group or person. There is nothing as good as accurate information in this part of the process.

Using the theory of the Force Field Analysis we now map out a strategy to use our strongest driving force while devising ways to decrease the strongest resisting force. The other forces are handled in the same way, until we are in a position to say: "Our first step will be. . . ." Second and third steps usually fall into place at this time.

If our planning has been well done, based on valid information and checked by others who know the situation, it will often be carried out substantially intact. But there could be misreadings, factors we overlooked, or new and unexpected forces that have entered the field. We need, then, to be flexible. Planning should not be a straitjacket; it is a guide. We stand back from it far enough and resist the temptation to "do it" at all costs if we find it is not working. If we are trying to bring about change, we need to be ready to change ourselves. We need to have the wisdom to know when to change our plans, or even our objective.

Why Planning Gets Grounded

One of the commonest reasons for planning not being done is simply that the need for it is not felt: "We don't have to go through all *that*!" As we want to jump to the solution in problem solving, so we want to jump to implementation in planning. "Just get it done" is the motto carved on many of our shields of battle. I would suggest that this is another indication of our denial of the Incarnation, except that it is a disease found also outside of church circles. Planning is, however, a very human need; it is like a road map that we refer to before we set out for a family vacation. The cost of ignoring it is to get lost.

But we are ingenious in developing ways to make planning difficult if not impossible. A friend of mine has made a list of these ways through the years, and I am sure it is only partial. All of us have heard the following at one time or another: "We tried that before." "Our place (parish, group, community) is different." "We're all too busy to do that." "It's too radical a change." "We don't have enough help (money, support)." "We've never done it that way before." "We're too small for that." "That's too ivory tower." "Why change? I thought we were doing O.K." "You can't teach an old dog new tricks." "Let's form a committee." "It's never been tried before." "Let's sleep on it." "You're two years ahead of your time," etc.

My friend calls such statements "Roadblocks to Creative Thinking and Action." Psychologists tell us that we are not able to think creatively and evaluatively at the same time. Perhaps planning is difficult for us because it calls for much of both kinds of thinking. Creativity is certainly involved in developing strategies to "get things off the ground"; evaluation is certainly required in the use of Force Field Analysis. The value of a structure for problem solving and for planning is that it provides time for both processes; it seems to me that it is the proper role of the leader to know how to provide such structures. Eventually, all who participate become skilled in the use of the structure; initially, the leader needs to know it so that he or she can introduce it.

Summary

Management consultants, especially those who work with church groups, regularly point out the importance of organization and planning; they point out that Moses had the people wandering in the desert for forty years, while Joshua, who succeeded Moses and created a tight organization of leaders and platoons, had the people in the Promised Land within a year or so! It is a cute parallel, given with "tongue in cheek," but it also happens to be true. Whether the organization was the *cause* of success, of course, is another question.

The fact is that many church groups and people feel that they are going around in circles, wandering about in the desert. I suggest that planning is worth a try to get to the Promised Land. The Detroit Conference, A Call to Action, more adroitly described the Promised Land than it gave a blueprint to its entry; official guidelines for religious education illuminate the goals and objectives, but leave the paths to them hidden in the woods; parish council guidelines legislate but do not tell us how to implement the legislation. This is true, at least, most of the time. And it is unavoidable.

Planning is a very "parochial" thing, affected by *our* particular kind of people, *our* resources, and *our* talents. There is no universal "How To" booklet; each group has to sweat it out for themselves. So let's stop our frantic convention searches for "How To" make my committee, parish, or community come alive. We have more than enough goals, objectives, ideals and dreams. Let's start the sweaty work of planning.

In this chapter we explored two methods of planning: the "management by objectives" or needs identification method, and the Force Field Analysis. We looked at some reasons why planning doesn't happen. Planning is the most alien of occupations to our church community in many areas of the world. For that reason, it is the greatest challenge the Christian leader has: to persuade his or her followers that planning is more than nice; it is necessary because it is the human path to accomplishment. And no one ever claimed, at least in so many words, that the Christian church was and is not human. Everyone who believes says that it is incarnational. Jesus obviously had a plan!

Chapter 8
Leadership and Management

There is a difference between leadership and management. Management is a particular kind of leadership. In their book *Management of Organizational Behavior*, Paul Hersey and Kenneth H. Blanchard state: "Leadership is a broader concept than management. Management is thought of as a special kind of leadership in which the accomplishment of organizational goals is paramount. The key difference between the two concepts, therefore, lies in the word *organization*." (Prentice Hall, Englewood Cliffs, N.J., 2nd ed., 1972, p. 5) In this light they define management as "working with and through individuals and groups to accomplish organizational goals." (*Ibid.*, p. 3) A leader, then, may attain his own goals, or help others to attain their personal goals, without being an effective manager. Management must be primarily directed to the attainment of the goals of the system or organization, the diocese, the parish, the church.

Peter Drucker, in his book *Management*, adds another dimension to management: its social responsibility. He says, "Every one (institution) is an organ of society and exists for the sake of society." (Harper & Row, N.Y., 1974, p. 41) Another dimension of management, then, is to manage the "social impacts and the social responsibilities of the enterprise." (*Ibid.*) No doubt this dimension of management is more acutely felt at higher levels of management, in the role of bishop or pastor, but it is a dimension that any Christian leader, whether of a prayer group, a parish council or a parish committee, would find useful to keep in mind. No system or organization exists in a vacuum; every significant decision, like a pebble tossed into a pond, makes ripples in the lives of other systems and organizations. As Christians we are the first to understand that "aloneness" is not possible: "If one part (of the body) is hurt, all parts are hurt with it. If one part is given special honor, all parts enjoy it." (1 Cor. 12:26) What is true of the human body and of Christ's body seems also to be true of the social body.

Management, therefore, can be an awesome task, especially if, finding ourselves in a leadership situation that calls for management skills, we have not been called upon to manage anything before. But that is not really true, since all of us have somehow managed our lives or our families. True, this is not the strict kind of management required in a community or organization, but a lot of the elements of management can be found in our everyday experience. We may not have reflected on them, and we may not have done as well as we could because we did not know some of the required elements of management, but, I believe, all of us can learn how to manage well.

What a Manager Needs To Do

A manager needs to plan, to organize, to motivate and to control. All of these functions are mutually dependent and may be pictured like this:

As the arrows indicate, they are not segmented activities, one coming to a complete close before the next step begins; rather, they are functions that are carried on more or less simultaneously, one, no doubt, taking precedence over the other at any given time, but all being regularly used all the time.

Planning, as we explored it in the last chapter, requires forecasting the availability and use of resources, people or material, as needed in the function of organizing. Planning looks to ways to motivate for the achievement of goals and objectives, especially involving those who will be needed to achieve them so that they may be motivated. It calls for preparing some way to determine the successful achievement of the goal or objective by setting up criteria and ways that progress will be reported, and that is controlling. All that was said in the last chapter is applicable here.

Organizing is the function of utilizing resources at our disposal in ways that will accomplish the task planned. It involves the proper utilization of the talents of those willing to cooperate in the venture, the use of the budget where it will help most and the use of materials that we have or that we can procure. Once the plan has been agreed upon, organization is the most urgent need of management. It is the "how" of the plan in action.

Motivating is the function of energizing ourselves or others to pursue a goal or objective. My experience with groups and group leadership indicates that it is the most obscure of management functions. Motivation arises out of a felt and acknowledged need. Put simply, if I feel hungry and acknowledge that I am hungry, I am motivated to prepare food and to eat it. The preparation of the food is called "goal directed activity"; the eating of the food is "goal activity." A need, therefore, offers a goal to me that affects my behavior for the fulfillment of the need.

Motivation, therefore, is the surfacing of a felt need. When discussing the value of group planning where a group was needed to implement the plan, I was simply pointing out one way to motivate: people will have a felt need to implement their own creations and ideas. The crux of motivation in planning is to allow others to contribute sufficiently so that they see the plan as their own, one in which they have a vested interest and to which they have a commitment. If a task can be done by myself alone, I do not have to have group planning since I do not need others for implementation. There is no need, then, for me to motivate others. If it is my plan, I shall have sufficient motivation to see it through. That is not to say that there is no value in utilizing the talents of others in developing my personal plans; they can add, and often do add, valuable insights I might have missed.

In chapter 1 I explained Abraham Maslow's theory of motivation, and it might be well to reread that section now (p. 9) if you do not recall it. The most valuable insight of Maslow is that no one is satisfied simply with goal activity. When the goal has been accomplished, we look around for other needs that call for fulfillment, that lead to goal directed behavior so that we may be able to engage in a new and different goal activity. The child of three, for instance, has crawled for months and struggled to learn to walk. Now that he or she can walk, now that he or she is in goal activity, that no longer motivates him or her; he or she feels a new need, for instance, to be able to give a reasonably connected story of an event in his or her life or to be able to follow two directions at once: "Go into the other room and get my sweater." When he or she is four years of age, he'll or she'll probably be doing these things, and they will no longer motivate him or her because he or she is doing them; he or she doesn't *need* to do them. His or her learning is motivated by need.

We never grow out of this process of motivation. People are motivated by need. To motivate, the manager either recognizes needs that are already present and call for satisfaction, or he or she is able to surface needs. The salesman or saleswoman knows how to surface needs, appealing to my need for uniqueness, for example, by pointing out: "This lamp is the only one of its kind. The craftsman or craftswoman has since died and he or she made only one!" All of us, including salesmen or saleswomen, know that such tactics are not always ethical, and that they sometimes motivate us to purchase what we truly can't afford. So, I am not talking about the Christian manager using unethical tactics. I am talking about his or her vision as a leader, the vision of which we spoke in chapter 2. There is a specific Christian leadership dimension to Christian management: the capacity to share a vision of possibility with others, or to help others develop their own vision. Such visions are born of Gospel reflection. In these kinds of visions are found the needs that are not yet felt and that the Christian manager can help to surface. The fruit of such visions often requires risk, but it is a risk we can afford.

Controlling is an odious term to many, and that, perhaps, is the reason why it is often the most neglected of managerial functions. We might do it more readily if we called it "follow-up" or some less tyrannical sounding word. In fact, controlling is nothing more than follow-up. The plan has been made, the resources have been organized, and the people involved have been motivated. It remains the responsibility of the manager to shepherd its completion: to make changes when experience warrants them, to support those who are giving time and energy to the task, to see that directives are being followed. In other words, it is not enough to give directions and walk away; the manager is there to see that they are being carried out. Controlling is a natural and painless function if planning, organizing and motivating have been done. It becomes painful when these three steps have been short-changed.

Styles of Management

The four functions of management are carried out in different ways by different managers. Most of us have developed our own ways of "handling things," so that we feel more comfortable managing things one way than another way. There are at least three distinct styles of management, and our particular management preference probably falls into one of these styles.

The *Traditional* manager is characterized by

strong commitment to the organization and reluctance to take risks.

The *Entrepreneurial* manager has little commitment to the organization and is excited by and quite willing to take risks, seeing them as challenges.

The *Purposeful* manager has strong commitment to the organization and is quite willing, at the same time, to experiment and take some risks.

A fourth style of management is sometimes cited and labeled "Crisis Management," characterized by little concern for the organization and resistance to taking risks. This manager is the "fire-fighter," constantly being required to handle crisis after crisis and regularly making decisions impulsively, "off the top of his or her head," because there is no planning. I see this as mismanagement or management by abdication. It is to be avoided, so I prefer not to waste time discussing it at length.

Each style of management has its own style of communication and its own approach to planning. The *Traditional* manager strongly favors bureaucracy because it is the surest way not to take risks; he or she also favors the use of clear and definite procedures that only rarely may be bypassed. His or her style of communication is *Controlling*, persuading and enforcing; he or she is strongly directive. His or her planning is usually confined by the way things have been done in the past and the use of groups in the organization as they now exist. Planning does not include much experimentation, or if there is experimentation and "trying new things" it usually involves only minor issues or functions of the organization. If such minor functions or issues become major, they are brought under tight control and strict procedures. Before the Second

Vatican Council, for instance, liturgy was a minor issue in the Roman Catholic Church; a great deal of experimentation was tolerated and not taken too seriously. It was generally ignored. The Second Vatican Council, however, made liturgy a major issue, so that official liturgical committees were established, a separate Vatican office was created, and decrees were issued on how far the experimentation with liturgy might go.

The *Entrepreneurial* manager works with short-range plans only, being quite willing to make the best use of opportunities as they arise. He or she is a speculator, hoping that "things work out in the end," and sometimes reveling in the risk taken. He or she communicates by *Relinquishing*, readily accommodating to others or complying with directives because they "come from the top." The Entrepreneurial manager feels little responsibility for the organization and is, therefore, open to take risks that might threaten the organization's vitality or life. It is the kind of management that generates vagueness of goals, uncertainty of purpose and confusion among the ranks. The functions of management are performed, but with such speed or ambiguity that they appear superficial or unnecessary or even as though they are not being performed. The group feels directionless, a direction being set this time by one opinion of a member and another time by another opinion of a member. Management doesn't seem to know what it wants.

The *Purposeful* manager plans systematically, in accord with preserving the life and vitality of the organization, and experimentally, seeing risk as a challenge to improve the quality (or quantity) of the organization. His or her planning is both long-range and short-range. The Purposeful manager's style of communication is *Developmental*. He or she shares information with others when it is appropriate, not only the amount of information he or she deems necessary for others to do their jobs, but as much as possible. He or she invites others to explore the issue and listens to their contributions. "This is what I know about this problem; let's explore it together and see what we can come up with" is his or her typical way of approaching an organizational issue. The Purposeful manager accepts responsibility but does not require that solutions always be his or her own; he or she is willing to become committed to a group decision that contains some elements of risk, but risk that has been examined responsibly.

The Traditional manager is the "back shot," looking at what has always been done before and choosing to do that now.

The Entrepreneurial manager is the "hot shot," changing directions at the slightest pressure and looking for immediate success—with flair.

The Purposeful manager is the "straight shot," having no hidden agendas and playing no games.

The crisis manager does not communicate, except by flight or by fight. He or she does not speak to the issue, if he or she speaks at all, but to the "persona": "You're always coming up with these screwy ideas!" If he or she can avoid the issue entirely, he or she is very happy. She or he is the "no shot."

While I have shown my preference for the Purposeful style of management, I believe that there can be times when both the Traditional style and the Entrepreneurial style can be effective. Cardinal Dougherty, Archbishop of Philadelphia from 1918 to 1951, was an example of a Traditional style of management during most of his ministry as a bishop, but it seems to me that he had to be an entrepreneur as he established the archdiocesan school system on solid financial footings. The Traditional style of our former President, Gerald Ford, seems to have been needed in the wake of the Entrepreneurial style of Richard Nixon. An effective style of management is not unlike an effective style of leadership as discussed in chapter 2: the situation or the issue often indicates the style that will be most effective.

A manager, like a leader, needs to judge the style of management that will be helpful in the particular situation he or she faces. What will be a successful style in Mother Teresa of India's situation might be highly ineffective in Northern Ireland. What is important is that the manager knows what style he or she is using and why.

Summary

Whether our service of management is in a prayer group, a parish council, a parish committee or a Vatican committee, the functions of management are the same: to plan, to organize, to motivate and to control. What style we use to perform those functions depends upon the needs of the group or organization, its size and age, as discussed in chapter 3, or its level of development, as discussed in that same chapter.

A Christian community needs good management as much as a purely secular community; our belief does not equip us with instant planning, instant organizing, instant motivation or wise controlling. These functions are filled with deeper meaning since they are directed to the coming of the Kingdom, but they are no easier or less required for that. In fact, if they are as important as I suspect, they are all the more required since so much is at stake.

The next chapter is a reflective one, a faith view of the relevance of human skills of leadership and relationships to the Christian mission. It is an investigation of the broad territory covered by Incarnational Theology. It is the reason I wrote this book.

Chapter 9
Christian Leadership

"Shouldn't we start with the Spirit, with a spiritual approach?" is a question I am frequently asked as I prepare to work with a Parish Council or Pastoral Team. My response is: "Why not start with the human as well as the spiritual?" It seems to me that since the believer is no less human for being spiritual, we cannot "start" with one without leaving the other aside. It is unfair (and unsuccessful, I believe) to deal with men and women as only souls or to deal with them as only intellects, emotions or bodies. If we are to grow at all, we grow humanly and spiritually. This is the message of the Incarnation, that our humanity is an integral part of salvation. The unbeliever may reject a spiritual dimension as an integral part of man or woman, since faith is a gift requiring our assent; the believer cannot reject the spiritual or the human dimensions. Once we believers accept faith in God, we carry with that assent all that is human. The story of Genesis declares that the only real world for the believer is the world created in the image of the Word, in the power of the Spirit, spoken by the Father.

The believer does not accept the reality of pure nature; it never existed. The world and man and woman were, from the beginning, created by the Word of God and bear His image: "He is the image of the unseen God and the first-born of all creation, for in

Him were created all things in heaven and on earth.
. . . He holds all things in unity." (Col. 1:15-16a & 17b)
Whether we deal with a board of directors of a business corporation, a neighborhood council, a parish
committee or a core group of a prayer group, we are
dealing with the same kind of human nature. Faith
makes that nature more meaningful, but it does not
change it. It seeks to free human nature from sin,
which was never and is not an integral part of its creation; faith restores human nature to its original creation, in Christ. It does not free human nature from its
fundamental character.

Robert Harvanek states this perspective suc-
cinctly:

> What, then, of the relevance of studies made in
> the business world to the world of religion? It
> could be objected that there is nothing farther
> apart in ethos and spirit than the business com-
> munity and the religious community, and there is
> some truth in this. At the same time, what the
> scientists have been investigating is the behavior
> of human nature in group and work situations, and
> though adjustment has to be made for different
> situations, enough evidence has been gathered
> from activity in very contrasting areas, military,
> educational, political and religious, as well as
> business, to judge that it is the same human nature
> operating in each. ("The Expectations of Leader-
> ship," *The Way*, vol. 15, no. 1, Jan. 1975, p. 22)

The behavioral and social sciences such as psychology, sociology and anthropology offer us a wealth of
insights into the human person. Revelation offers a

wealth of insight into the human person. It seems reasonable that, since both these human sciences and divine revelation have the same focal point, the human person, it is useful to listen to what both have to say about their common subject.

Leadership and Process

In this light of the overlapping of the human sciences and divine revelation, Christian leadership is only one element. It is different from secular leadership in that it is expected to have a faith vision, a specific mission of influencing the activities of an individual or group in efforts toward accomplishing goals that contribute to the coming of the Kingdom of God. It is the same as secular leadership insofar as the individuals and groups it leads remain human, just as the leader does.

As long as we are human, growth and development require change, a constant "being in process." Leadership, like all that is human, can be improved; the Christian leader is called to improve both spiritually and humanly simultaneously. His or her faith must deepen as his or her leadership skills are bettered. "Virtue stands in the middle," the Fathers of the Church often proclaimed. Christian leadership shares that spot: to develop spiritually and not humanly is to court "spiritism" which discounts the human; to develop humanly and not spiritually is to court "humanism" which discounts the Spirit.

God who made us knows best our need to grow and develop, to be in process, if we are to live. His way of dealing with us, His style of leadership, changed as our growth in salvation changed. With Abraham, God was a Father, a parent to be trusted, a God who was almighty, powerful and faithful. When Israel needed disciplining, God's leadership took on the role of the strict parent and lawgiver. In both of these early theophanies God used a leadership style of High Task; with Abraham He used High Relationship as well; with Israel His style also employed Low Relationship as He recalled them to their purpose for existence.

In time, through the prophets Amos and Osee, God revealed Himself as husband and intimate lover of His People. Jesus confirmed this relationship by calling Himself the bridegroom in the Gospels. His style of leadership often tended to Low Task and High Relationship, although His own sense of mission was none the less for that. The point is that God revealed Himself in process, as His People were prepared for a deepening relationship. Had He revealed Himself as lover and husband too early, when Israel was in need of a directive disciplinarian, His love might have been taken for weakness; His leadership most probably would have been misunderstood and been ineffective.

In this sense the Christian leader, clergy or lay, has a model in Scripture. It is a model of process, requiring the kind of judgment discussed in chapter 2, more than a potter's mold. It calls for the human skills explored in this book, the development of skills that will supply the needs of the community as the leader correctly perceives them. Leadership requires growth, since no one is born with all the skills that leadership requires; Christian leadership requires spiritual as well as human skills, one no less than the other.

Other implications are that we need to be patient with ourselves and with others. Process implies that growth and development are in progress: some are at one level of relationship with God, others at another; we have the skills to make some effective decisions about the kind of leadership needed now, but we lack some skills also, so that sometimes our perceptions and judgments are ineffective. Realizing that we are in process, we can learn from our experience, from both successful and failure experiences. We are not doomed to have one year's experience fifty times, but wise enough to have fifty years of experience.

Leadership and Relationship

Relationship is the key to understanding leadership, since leadership always involves relationships with others, others who perceive the leader as leader if his or her leadership is effective. From a human viewpoint, this is the reason why so much of this book has been an exploration of human relationships; from the divine viewpoint, man or woman is not truly man or woman unless he or she is in relationship to God and to others.

God Himself is relational, the very names of Father, Son and Spirit indicating relationships. Because of His relationship to the Son, the Father is a father, begetting His Son from all eternity. The Personhood of the Son is totally relational, being Himself only in relationship with the Father. The Spirit is the personified relationship of Love between Father and Son; His being itself is the relational being of Love.

Because man or woman is made in the image and likeness of God, he or she too is fundamentally and operationally a relational being. A person becomes himself or herself in relationship with others—parents, friends, co-workers, etc. We know that an infant will die if left without human touch or companionship, although his or her other physical needs for food, hygiene, etc., are adequately supplied. Many of us, as we have discussed or exchanged ideas with others, have found out things about ourselves that were quite important, but would have remained hidden without the observations of another. We need only recall chapter 5 on "feedback" to remind ourselves of the importance of seeing ourselves as others see us.

The Christian faith itself is relational. James W. Fowler of Harvard has pointed out that faith is relational in our *sense of relatedness* to the transcendent, in our case to God Himself. He says further that faith carries with it a relationship to the community, the believing community in the case of the Christian believer. It is the believing community, as noted in chapter 6, that preserves and penetrates revelation. Even if I do not adhere to a particular Christian community, my Christian faith has come to me through the Christian community in its widest sense. (See Thomas Hennessy, ed., *Values and Moral Development*, Paulist Press, N.Y., 1976, p. 175)

The Christian leader cannot ignore the human demands of relationship with those whom he or she leads. Jesus acknowledged those demands by becoming man, "like us in all things but sin." (Eucharistic Prayer IV) He chose to place Himself within human relationships, within human community, so that sin might be conquered; He knew that only He and those whom He related to Himself could live sinless in a sinful world. He used human skills to bring human salvation. The Christian leader cannot escape this model, the Incarnate model that placed paramount importance upon the human need for relationships. True, Jesus calls us to transcend the human, to look to the Kingdom, to pray. But He also says to love one another visibly, for all to see, and that calls for human skills of caring and concern appropriately! For the Christian leader, "appropriately" is the key word: to know what to give and when to give it for an appropriate manifestation of love, the Christian leader needs to have the human insight to see real needs and the human skill to meet those needs.

Jesus is not a mold into which the Christian leader pours himself or herself but an exemplar to be recalled and applied in this particular situation at this particular time. It is His Spirit that the Christian leader must allow to act, not a replay of His life. I contend that only the Christian leader who has the human skills of leadership can give the Spirit of Jesus full rein.

Leadership: Clerical and Lay

Since beginning this book I have found a question regularly coming to mind. It is not one of those asked in the first paragraph of the first chapter, which have all been addressed. It is the question: "What is the difference between clerical and lay leadership, if any?"

To answer this question we need to reflect a bit on the history of the clerical state. One prominent theologian has said: "There is no direct link between the contemporary offices of the Church (the episcopate, the presbyterate and the diaconate) and an act of institution on the part of Jesus while he was on earth." (Edward Schillebeeckx, "Catholic Understanding of

Office," *Theological Studies*, vol. 30, no. 4, December 1969, p. 568) An historical study of the clerical state reveals that only after a century or more had passed after the death of the last of Christ's Apostles did the term "priest" enter the Christian vocabulary. It may have been avoided up to that time to avoid confusion with the pagan priesthoods so common in the early life of the Church. In the *Didache*, one of the earliest of our post Gospel documents, "prophets" and "teachers" were the preferred presidents of the Eucharistic celebration. Overseers, the original meaning of "episcopoi" or bishops, celebrated only if a prophet or teacher was not present! By the third century, however, "priest" was a name applied to a bishop; by the fourth century the residence of the priest became a "holy place." From that time on the priesthood took on more and more of a ritualistic function, Isidore of Seville in the seventh century giving first place among priestly tasks to the "confection of the divine body and blood." Peter Lombard and the great Scholastic theologians of the twelfth and thirteenth centuries, St. Thomas Aquinas, St. Bonaventure and St. Albert the Great, followed the lead of Isidore of Seville.

Very early Christianity used the term "laity" to include *all* Christians, the Christian community, thereby reflecting the biblical tradition of the Old Testament in which Israel was God's "laos," God's People, and its fulfillment in the New Testament where "laos," laity, referred to the Church. (Cf. Mt. 1:21; 2:6; 2 Cor. 6:16; Acts 15:14) Clement of Rome, Justin, Origen and Tertullian of the second century were the first to distinguish the "president" of the Eucharistic Assembly from the laity and to speak of "ministers" as distinct from laity. Up until then the laity included all baptized Christians.

In short, there is a long Christian tradition that attributes a special kind of leadership to the clerical state. Karl Rahner, S.J. balances the earlier and later views of this leadership by defining a priest as "he who, related to an at least potential community, preaches the Word of God by mandate of the Church as a whole and therefore officially, and in such a way that he is entrusted with the highest levels of sacramental intensity of this Word." ("A Definition of the Priestly Ministry," *Concilium*, Paulist Press, vol. 43, p. 83) Rahner views the Sacraments as well as the verbal preaching of the Gospel as proclamations of the Word of God in the sense of St. Paul who said: "Until the Lord comes . . . every time you eat this bread and drink this cup, you are proclaiming His death. . . ." (1 Cor. 11:26)

The medieval view of the priesthood tended to emphasize the ritualistic, sacramental role of the priest. Since sacraments are central to Christian life, it is not surprising that the priesthood tended also to dominate administration and decision making in the community. Such a perspective makes it difficult to fulfill many of the expectations of present-day leadership, such expectations as explored in this book. Rahner and other recent theologians have suggested a perspective of the priesthood that is more authentically traditional while also being adaptable to the needs of any culture or age. The clerical leadership is found principally in being set apart for that understanding of the Gospel that is proclaimed in Word and Sacrament for the unifying and building of the Church. It can go further, giving even wider service through committee work and administration, but that is because the cleric has talent, not because he is ordained.

The Second Vatican Council persistently pointed

up the responsibility of the laity to assume leadership roles: "Christ's redemptive work, while of itself directed toward salvation of men and women, involves also the renewal of the whole temporal order. . . . In fulfilling this mission of the Church, the laity, therefore, exercise their apostolate both in the Church and in the world." (*Decree on the Apostolate of the Laity*, par. 5) Shortly after this statement the Council became even more precise: "The laity should accustom themselves to working in the parish in close union with their priests, bringing to the church community their own and the world's problems as well as questions concerning human salvation, all of which should be examined and resolved by common deliberation." (*Ibid.* par. 10)

Strangely enough, one of the major obstacles to a fuller and more responsible lay leadership in the Church is the distorted understanding of the priesthood (the episcopate, the diaconate) that we have inherited. The father image of the priest tends to allow us to be irresponsible, perhaps even to support "Father's" misunderstanding of his own role in the Church. There needs to be a better understanding of authentic Church leadership on both sides.

Once we have clarified this theological issue, there is greater likelihood that both cleric and layperson will take the Incarnation seriously, recognizing the need of the human skills of leadership both for the baptized and the ordained Christian. We take the Incarnation seriously when we accept our humanity, admitting that we do need to take seriously the behavioral sciences, psychology, sociology and anthropology when they share with us their findings about the working of human nature. We take the Incarnation seriously when we recognize that the Spirit usually works through us, taking us as we are, and that, therefore, we can facilitate His work by becoming more humanly skillful.

The answer to the question, then, about the difference between clerical and lay leadership is that it differs in the *kind* of service given, the clerical serving the community with the proclamation of the Word, the lay serving the community by supplying the functions needed to allow it to be the effective priest of the world, the reconciler and witness to the Lord and all that He can do. The *quality* of the leadership, whether clerical or lay, is dependent upon the acquiring and application of human skills, be they study, meditation, reflection, preaching or group dynamics. If the skills are not acquired, the price is mutual dissatisfaction, the layman or laywoman staying away from "church," and the priest discouraging lay participation in parish or diocesan affairs.

Our Church has within it all the means to bring about the Kingdom, the seeds of the fullness to which God calls the world through Christ. We need only to get it together, to use what we have, to develop what we need, and to rejoice in our working together and working with the Lord.

Summary

The effective leader is in a constant process of development, learning from his or her experience. He or she is content with process, because he or she recognizes perfection as something always to be achieved. The search is exciting, modeled as it is upon God's own interventions, gradually and sensitively, into our human history.

The effective leader knows how to treat people, to recognize needs and to fulfill those needs (or at least to let others know that he or she sees them as important). He or she accepts human nature as essentially relational, made, as we are, in the image and likeness of a relational God. He or she knows how to get jobs done while helping people to feel their worth.

The effective leader who is Christian, be he or she clerical or lay, accepts seriously all the demands of process and relationship, while sharing with others a vision of the Kingdom for whose coming the Church exists. He or she recognizes the special calling and talents of each person, the special function of the priesthood, of the religious life, of the layman or the laywoman, without exalting one to the disparagement of the others and without confusing one with the other. He or she appreciates the richness of diversity and helps others to do the same.

The effective Christian leader is not a superman or superwoman, expected to be greater than the Master who chose to redeem the world through human nature. He or she accepts things as they are, while keeping a burning desire to better everything "through Christ, with Christ and in Christ." And like Christ, he or she will use all that is truly human to manifest the divine.